THE GAIA PROJECT

About the Author

Hwee-Yong Jang, PhD, is a business professor in South Korea who earned advanced degrees at the University of Minnesota and at Purdue University.

Dr. Jang began *gi* (energy) practice in late 1997 because of a health problem. As a result of this practice, he experienced a dramatic expansion of consciousness.

Hoping that other people might experience consciousness expansion from an understanding of the intangible energy world, Dr. Jang wrote his first book, entitled *What We See Is Not the Only Truth*, in 2000.

Dr. Jang's spiritual experiences—including past-life regression, channeling, dreaming, and energy reading—stimulated his continuous self-awakening and led him to fully understand the Gaia Project.

Please visit Dr. Jang's website at: www.gaiaproject.co.kr.

HWEE-YONG JANG

THE
G A I A
PROJECT
2012:
THE EARTH'S COMING GREAT CHANGES

TRANSLATED BY MIRA TYSON

Llewellyn Publications
Woodbury, Minnesota

The Gaia Project 2012: The Earth's Coming Great Changes © 2007 by Hwee-Yong Jang. All rights reserved. No part of this book may be used or reproduced in any manner whatsoever, including Internet usage, without written permission from Llewellyn Publications except in the case of brief quotations embodied in critical articles and reviews.

Original Korean title: *Gaia Project*

Book design by Steffani Chambers
Cover design by Kevin R. Brown
Cover image © 2007 Photodisc
Edited by Brett Fechheimer
Translated from the Korean by Mira Tyson

ISBN-13: 978-0-7387-1042-6

Llewellyn Worldwide does not participate in, endorse, or have any authority or responsibility concerning private business transactions between our authors and the public.

All mail addressed to the author is forwarded but the publisher cannot, unless specifically instructed by the author, give out an address or phone number.

Any Internet references contained in this work are current at publication time, but the publisher cannot guarantee that a specific location will continue to be maintained. Please refer to the publisher's website for links to authors' websites and other sources.

Llewellyn Publications
2143 Wooddale Drive, Dept. 0-7387-1042-3
Woodbury, MN 55125-2989, U.S.A.

Printed in the United States of America

Acknowledgments

First of all, I would like to thank those who made efforts to bring this book to the world, including Mira Tyson and my daughter, Christine, who participated in the translation work. I extend my gratitude to the staff of Llewellyn Publications—especially Nanette Peterson, Brett Fechheimer, Kevin R. Brown, and Steffani Chambers—for their unwavering support and efforts. Also, I am grateful to Joon Sik Park, Jin-Woo Kim, and Min Kyung Sung for their assistance in revising and editing the manuscript, as well as to a few people who first helped me write the Korean-language version of this book.

Furthermore, my great thanks go to various beings, especially the Consciousness of the Earth, who helped me escape from the quagmire of oblivion and restore my original state. In addition, I wholeheartedly thank every being on the earth, all of whom have traveled a long way together to "Oneness," and I sincerely hope that they realize, during the short remaining time on the earth, that we are all "one that originated from one source."

Contents

Preface

Everyone encounters turning points in their lives. I have experienced several in my lifetime, but the most crucial one came in my late forties, when my life shifted gears and took on a whole new direction and meaning.

After having maintained a stable, well-adjusted life in this material world without much difficulty, a sudden heart problem came as a tremendous shock to me during the summer of 1996. This shock made me question my priorities and values in life, and resurrected confusion I'd had as a teenager regarding the meaning of life and its origins. I was desperate to find a means out of this confusion and restlessness, and this wandering eventually led me, beginning in the autumn of 1997, to practice meditation and other breathing methods. This course of action changed my mind and body at a fundamental level, and finally led me to write this book.

After I started practicing *gi,* a term referring to the natural energy that composes the universe, my *hyeol,* which are spots on the body suitable for acupuncture, began to open.

I started to sense the *gi* that surrounded my body, and I subtly came to realize that this energy must be a more fundamental basis for my being, more so than my physical body. Recognizing the invisible world for the first time in my life, I measured various energy levels with an L-rod, the tool commonly used to detect underground water streams. Doing so helped me to understand a great deal about human consciousness and consciousness levels. As the energy of the universe poured into my body continuously, my mind remained in perpetual and unconditional peace. I no longer desired fame or fortune, and I was virtually unattached to material possessions.

I began to write *What We See Is Not the Only Truth* during the autumn of 2000, hoping that readers might be able to experience a significant change in consciousness through an understanding of the energy world. The book was published the following spring, and I started my website, www.fortruth.net, around that time as well. Both events enabled me to meet many people with similar interests in spirituality.

These interactions with spiritual people gave me a more certain and concrete understanding of the invisible world. I began to understand how *gi* is piloted through the mind and how spiritual abilities come into manifestation. I even started to understand other various phenomena associated with *gi*—including ghosts, possession, and the spiritual world after death. As a result of these many unusual experiences, I understood the relationship between past and present lives. By trying past-life regressions on people, the concept of reincarnation became clear as well. The fundamental question of "What am I doing here?" was answered by messages delivered in these various ways, as well as through my continuous self-awakening. That was when the feeling of the earth's "Great Change" started kindling inside of me.

As the truth about life, the earth, and the entire universe—which had been hidden in dense fog until then—began to be revealed, I sighed and asked myself, "The real world seems to be explained in a simple way. Why haven't we humans realized this until now?" Upon finishing this book, I am clear about how this world will go on. And, without a doubt, I understand what this book will accomplish and how much impact it will have on people on the earth.

When I was writing *What We See Is Not the Only Truth*, I focused on convincing a wide audience about the existence of the invisible world, and on easily and systematically explaining the energy world to this audience. However, in retrospect, I now feel that my first book was a bit too obvious: not because I expect that most people will accept the contents of that book with natural ease, but because, relative to this new book, *What We See Is Not the Only Truth* is much more likely to be understood and accepted by the general public. To people who have lived their lives without asking themselves why they are alive, this new book—which provides a clear picture of humans, the earth, and the universe—could be considered "nonsense" as well.

The contents of this book go far beyond established concepts and knowledge, and readers who are not familiar with the writings on my website might experience quite a bit of confusion at first. Not only readers who are entirely unfamiliar with the energy world, but also spiritual or religious people who are relatively familiar with concepts such as gi, meditation, the soul, spirits, the spiritual world, clairvoyance, ESP, past lives, and reincarnation could be quite perplexed. Readers who understand the invisible energy world pretty well, who accept the existence of extraterrestrials and UFOs, and who have read various channeling books, could even face the same kind of confusion.

During a visit to Los Angeles in the summer of 2004, I tried past life regressions on eager participants. In unison, all of them saw their existence being shifted to Sirius, the brightest star in the night sky. Vivid scenes of life on Sirius were presented to them in terms more real than what they'd see on a movie screen. They also felt my presence alongside them on the star.

Understandably, these participants were awed and shocked afterward, since they are ordinary businesspeople and homemakers who had no advance knowledge of the spiritual world. I was told later that they compared the images they had seen, had a long discussion among themselves, and voiced suspicion that I might have somehow manipulated them into seeing those images.

A similar shock might occur to anyone who reads this book. Some readers might be stunned or shocked because the information in this book is so different from existing knowledge about the world. Readers may be especially surprised when they read about the extraordinary cosmic plan called the "Gaia Project" and the new complete history of the earth contained in this book. Perhaps some might suspect that the contents of this book are mere fabrications from my imagination. However, regardless of what readers might initially think, everything in this book will be revealed little by little as truth, and in the near future many people will begin to accept this book as a special message.

If you feel drawn to this book, I recommend reading it over and over again. Regardless of whatever spin on life you may have, whatever religious views you may hold, or whatever sacred texts you hold up as truth, I cannot emphasize enough the importance of understanding this book. Here is the truth of the universe presented to all the people on the earth in preparation for the Great Change.

Hwee-Yong Jang
January 2006
Incheon, Korea, Earth

AS I BEGIN THIS BOOK . . .

When I was a little boy, I once had the chance to watch a well being cleaned out in the front yard of my family's home. My father felt that the pollution level in the well was no longer acceptable, and so he decided to hire a few workers to clean it out. They began the process by bailing all the water out of the well, one bucket at a time. The well always seemed to be full, even during dry periods, but it began to show its floor after the men emptied it with the well buckets for a while.

One worker entered its hollow passage and returned with shoes, paper, toothbrushes, and other miscellaneous objects that had fallen into the hole over the years. Watching the man being pulled up by a rope, I felt an urge to follow his example and go into the well. After much persuasion, I was granted permission to do so. I got in the bucket as the men carefully lowered me down to the bottom of the well.

The cleaning process was already over and the well was in a satisfactory state with only a few puddles of clear water here and there. Inside the well, I felt as if I were on a vacation to a creek. I picked up pebbles, rubbed the moss stuck between rocks, and generally entertained myself. Moments later, I raised my head and saw the grand wall of stones piled up above me, and the small circle of blue sky peeking through the well's entrance. Suddenly, I felt an overwhelming tidal wave of confinement, oppression, and fear. I yelled to be pulled back up and the workers answered my call.

"Frogs in a well" is a well-known Korean saying, referring to limited awareness of a bigger world. A frog born in a well will only know about life in that well, and will never suspect anything outside of the well that he cannot perceive. Imagine that this frog is intuitive, with the gift of a sixth sense. He could tell stories about an outside world, but his frog friends would most likely deny such outrageous claims. And even those frogs who do feel the existence of a bigger world would feel overwhelmed by their immediate reality and their uncertainty over matters that they cannot physically experience—so they will mostly be persuaded by the other frogs to ignore such impracticalities.

Human beings have persisted in thinking and understanding in this way—as if they were frogs in a well—until now. Despite globalization, rapid transportation, and high-speed communication, there still may be some people, living in the same small town all of their lives, who expect people outside their town to be somehow different from themselves. People who have never had any contact with outsiders might even believe that those of a different race have different internal organs, or they might suspect that their blood is not even red. And even those people who understand humanity's tendency to be like frogs in a well are still limited in their perceptions by the five senses, and are, in general, extremely hesitant to accept new concepts and new facts.

It is true that various fields of science—especially quantum theory and astrophysics, which deal with the smallest and largest matters—have helped people overcome their conservative tendencies. During the last century, astronomy and astrophysics have provided people with a continuous stream of new and interesting knowledge, and have changed the general public's perception of the universe. As a result, humans are now very aware that both the sun and the earth are like tiny specks of sand compared to the size of the entire universe.

However, this expansion of understanding has mainly been superficial and, in fact, the public's way of thinking has not really changed much from that of people in the Middle Ages, who believed that the whole universe revolved around the earth. Like those who believed the sun circles the earth, we still have the same egocentric and human-oriented mentality. For example, rationally speaking, there is no possibility of life forms being limited to the earth in this infinite universe, but that is still a hard fact for many people to swallow. Even though UFOs are being caught on camera or seen with naked eyes at this very moment, most people still deny the existence of UFOs. Even those who admit to their presence may still imagine aliens to be monsters in shape and form.

Some might argue that it is no big deal that people have prejudices and a limited understanding of the world since that has always been the human condition. However, when people believed that the sun rotated around the earth, this limited understanding was not a problem because no one could build rockets to travel into space then. When people thought there were cliffs that fell into hell just beyond the horizon, it was not a problem because no one had the ability to sail to distant countries then. None of these beliefs caused any difficulties or discomfort in people's everyday lives. Similarly, as long as humans don't need to travel into space or communicate with beings outside of the earth, thinking like a frog in a well won't cause people any discomfort.

Humanity has now reached a very special point in history, different from any other time in the past, when we must understand our lives and our world with certainty. Until now, our limited information and deeply rooted prejudices have allowed us to ignore the truth and rules of the universe, and doing so has neither blocked our pursuit of happiness nor become an obstacle in our daily lives. But we are now at a turning point, where conveniently standing by blindfolded is no longer acceptable. It is time for humankind to shed the ignorance it has had for so long about itself and the universe. If we can't, it is possible that the meaning of life itself will vanish. Indeed, human beings are now facing the most crucial turning point in history.

This book will discuss an enormous cosmic project called the "Gaia Project." The Project is an unprecedented huge-scale plan even in the unlimited universe, and the earth is at the center of the plan. It includes the initial formation and the final change of the earth, which is called in this book the earth's "Great Change." Although this book discusses the fundamental purpose, process, and influence of the Project in detail, the focus of this book is on the Project's final stage: the Great Change, currently in full-scale progress. This book explains why the Great Change, which most of the general public may consider catastrophic or the end of the world, is happening, and it explains what changes will accompany the Great Change, and what humanity will experience and learn from the process. For an explanation of how this book was written, and how the information in it was received, please see chapter 9.

By reading this book and gaining an understanding of what is now occurring on this planet, people—including you—can prepare for the upcoming changes. In other words, when people begin to accept the facts clarified in this book with open minds, their understanding of life, the earth, and the universe will expand dramatically and they will be able to accept the outside changes with a sense of peace, even experiencing the joy of being together during the cosmic festivities on the earth.

In that respect, this book can be considered a summary of the Gaia Project and the scripture clarifying the origin and nature of the earth and humans from the cosmic point of view. Also, this book will be *the* book that everyone experiencing the extraordinary changes must read: that is, the guidebook to the earth's Great Change.

PART ONE
THE GAIA PROJECT

INTRODUCTION TO PART ONE

Most phenomena that occur on the earth or in the universe have been considered to have happened accidentally or by chance. This sentiment eliminates any possibility that there might be any intention or purpose behind those phenomena. Natural disasters such as volcanic eruptions, earthquakes, and hurricanes are considered accidental, and the formation of the earth as well as the sun is also frequently thought of in this manner. In other words, people commonly believe that there is no "why" to nature.

Recent theories such as chaos theory and fractal theory point out that there are certain rules even for phenomena that appear to be fortuitous or random, suggesting that there might be hidden intentions behind such phenomena. However, modern scientists reject the idea of a higher being who controls nature, including events such as changes in the weather and the occurrence of sunspots, as they attempt to distance themselves from folk culture and religion. Even though scientists attempt to find the formula, order, or system that creates certain phenomena, they do not sense the possibility that these systems might be created or changed for a reason. In other words, based on analysis and estimation of certain phenomena, modern science might have found order to a certain extent, but it seems far from finding basic causes and intentions.

According to the explanations of modern science, the earth and all its living forms were created by chance and have been gradually evolving ever since. Scientists believe that humans, the highest grade of life form on the earth, were also created in the same way and have also been evolving ever since. On the other hand, there are some religions that insist that everything was created by divine providence. Due to their lack of systemization and rationality, however, such religious insistence is, on its own merits, neither convincing nor easily accepted by non-believers.

However, since the whole universe was created and unfolded by the consciousness of the Origin, there is an intention or reason behind every phenomenon occurring in the universe. Contrary to most people's expectations, there are no phenomena that happen accidentally or by chance. In this respect, when people call a phenomenon "natural," they are merely implying that it is impossible for them to determine the reason or intention behind it. The Gaia Project, for which a special planet was created and changed intentionally, clearly shows how the universe is operated.

In Part One, I first present an outline of the Gaia Project, including its purpose, its steps, and its characteristics. I also explain the last step of the Project—i.e., the Great Change of the earth—in detail. In addition, I discuss the role of the Guides who were sent to the earth for missions related to the Project.

CHAPTER ONE
Outline of the Gaia Project

The term "Gaia Project" (or simply "the Project") may sound very strange to most readers, except for people who have visited my website and have read segments of my "Meditation Records." The word "Gaia" first appeared in Greek mythology, referring to the earth goddess and later to "the self-controlling organic earth." Anyone who knows the meaning of the term might guess that Gaia Project is a sort of space project related to the earth, but soon might ask, "What kind of nonsense are you talking about?"

So far, the general public has not even recognized the possibility of highly developed life forms, similar to human beings, on other planets. When they hear that the universe is involved in changing and refreshing the earth and when they read about a huge cosmic operation relating to the earth, they may consider such information to be a hoax or merely science fiction. It's difficult for them to accept the idea that the earth was formed for a special purpose and that it has been operated under careful supervision of high-dimensional beings. Even people who accept the existence of highly intelligent life forms in outer space probably find it difficult to imagine that there are beings that give direct orders for running the earth. For that reason, people might guess that the Gaia Project must be a humorous, odd, or exaggerated expression for significant changes taking place on the earth.

However, regardless of popular opinions, there are in fact many beings who have taken part directly and indirectly in the operation of the earth since its formation, and there are many beings who have been sent to the earth for missions related to the Great Change. The Gaia Project, which includes all the plans from the earth's formation to its ascension to the fifth dimension, does really exist. Thus, if we understand the Gaia Project in its entirety, we not only know the history of the earth and its living beings, but we also naturally develop insight into humankind.

The Gaia Project refers to a universe-wide plan related to the earth, one that has been carried out for a very long time. To understand the Gaia Project better, it may be necessary to have some basic background knowledge regarding how the universe is constituted and operated. The universe is mostly not materialized and is very different from the material earth, so that describing or explaining the universe in any human language is not an easy job at all. People on the earth can only roughly imagine the universe. With this fact in mind, only a brief explanation of the cosmic constitution and movement is presented here. As a related issue, chapter 7 explains how "being," or "consciousness," was originated.

Formation and Movement of the Universe

All things in the universe vibrate with their own frequencies. The universe is unfolded in such a manner that different worlds with different dimensions coexist simultaneously. Unlike notions of dimensions in mathematics and physics, a dimension in the universe indicates a band of vibration frequencies. The universe consists of ten dimensions: from the tenth dimension, with the highest frequencies, to the first dimension, with the lowest frequencies.

Everyone and everything in the universe belongs to one of the dimensions. Everything in the universe is laid out by the vibration of the tenth dimension, whose frequency is high enough to hold all of the information of the universe. As the frequencies get farther away from the origin of the universe, they gradually become lower and their roles become simpler. Even within the same dimension, there is quite a difference in frequency, and thus each dimension can be divided again into layers. These differences in dimension cause variations in terms of functions, purposes, and ways of existence, and the basic order of the universe can be said to be based on dimensions, or frequencies.

There are close to seven hundred galaxies in the unfolded universe. This number is vastly different from the one estimated by astrophysicists—tens of millions of galaxies. This difference comes from the fact that the stars, galaxies, and the universe that modern scientists observe are quite different from the real picture. The observation devices used by scientists sense light and waves belonging only to the material domain, so the worlds they recognize are different from the universe, which mostly belongs to the non-material domain. Thus, there is naturally a huge gap between the number of galaxies estimated by scientists and the number revealed here.

Each galaxy has its own formation principles and operation system, as well as its own inherent rules. Each galaxy, administered by beings of eighth- or ninth-dimensional frequencies, consists of several dimensions and is comprised of many stars with different characteristics. Each star has a particular dimensional frequency with its own unique function and mission. For instance, a certain star serves as the headquarters for a certain galaxy, while another star functions as a place of learning or as a library for a certain level of the universe. A star cluster can be composed of stars with the same or different dimensions.

In the tenth dimension, which has the highest frequency of vibration, there are five beings from the Origin of the universe, who are called in this book the "first consciousnesses of the universe," the "consciousnesses of the Origin," the "beings of the Origin," or, simply, the tenth-dimensional beings. They do not stay on a particular star, but instead spread out throughout the universe at all times in the form of light.

The relationship among the five beings of the Origin is like a brotherhood or sisterhood. Since each possesses somewhat different characteristics and qualities, some differences exist in their roles.

The first Origin, blue in its representative color, has the most masculine energy and is characterized by expansion and progression. The second Origin, magenta in color, has the most feminine energy, and is characterized by caring, harmony, and intercommunication among beings. The third Origin, a cool turquoise in color, has the most calm and quiet energy of the five Origins, and is characterized by pureness, fairness, unity, and wholeness. The Gaia Project has been conceived and is being unfolded by this being of the Origin. The fourth Origin, solid gold in color, is characterized by construction, realization and specification. The fifth Origin, an endless black in color, is characterized by stillness, quietness, and reflection. The beings once incarnated as Buddha and Christ were both created by this being of the Origin.

Unlike the beings of the Origin, all the other beings stay on a particular star. Each of them resides on a star with an appropriate frequency for various purposes. As mentioned before, some beings work to administer a star or galaxy or to carry out certain functions, and others may simply stay on a star to experience and learn. However, there is never a case when one being stays in one place permanently. Once a mission is accomplished or an experience is fulfilled, the beings move to another star or planet.

Within a galaxy in the same dimension, it is possible to move or travel from one star to another without restrictions. But it is generally impossible to move to a different dimensional world. On some stars, beings from different dimensions can coexist with the aid of special equipment that adjusts frequencies. Broadly analogous to immigration controls on the earth, traveling from one star to another requires beings to pass through a star gate. In a similar fashion, beings have to pass through a more strictly controlled gate in order to move from one galaxy to another. Since the free will of all beings comes into prior consideration, every operation reflects the will of related beings. However, no matter which galaxy or star they are staying on, beings have to follow the rules.

Due to unique birth processes and experiences, each being has a different frequency, has different abilities, and possesses different characteristics. Usually those with similar frequencies and characteristics stay on the same star. Each star has its own rules and systems, and governs itself independently unless the rules of its own galaxy or of higher dimensions are violated. In some exceptional cases, higher-dimensional beings can interfere. Among the innumerable events happening throughout the universe, there are projects planned and carried out throughout the entire universe. The Gaia Project, which people on the earth are now experiencing, represents one of these projects.

Frequencies, Dimensions, and Roles

All beings in the universe vibrate, and beings that vibrate have consciousness—in other words, an ability to perceive, no matter how weak. This perception capacity is determined by the being's frequency. As anyone who has studied wave theory knows, a wave's frequency of vibration determines how much information the wave can hold. A higher frequency has a higher information storage capacity. So, a being with a higher frequency level can hold more information, and therefore has a greater capacity to recognize and understand the world.

The frequency of the tenth dimension, which is the frequency of the Origin of the universe, has the capacity to hold the entire information of the universe. For this reason, tenth-dimensional beings are able to perceive everything that is happening in the universe. Compared with tenth-dimensional beings, ninth-dimensional beings can hold a relatively limited amount of information, so they understand only a segment of the universe: for example, everything about a certain galaxy or about the place under the being's control. Of course, a being of the eighth dimension holds less information compared to ninth-dimensional beings, as its frequency is lower. The amount of information held by beings of the seventh dimension or the sixth dimension can be explained in the same manner, with the capacity to hold information decreasing rapidly as the dimension decreases.

A being's role naturally differs depending on its frequency and its capacity to store information. In general, the lower the dimension of the being, the simpler its function and role. The supervision of the entire universe can be handled only by the beings of the Origin, who can hold all the information of the universe, while the management of certain regions can be delegated to those of lower frequencies.

The ninth-dimensional beings are usually involved in managing galaxies and stars, and in keeping law and order in the universe. While tenth-dimensional beings are directly related to the creation of the universe itself and to all of the beings in the universe, ninth-dimensional beings maintain the structural format of the universe and carry out the absolute laws of the universe.

Eighth-dimensional beings are similar to ninth-dimensional beings in terms of having leadership responsibilities, but their roles are somewhat limited and more specific. Seventh-dimensional beings are usually related to construction and creation; engineering and design are accomplished within this dimension, and the specific technology of creating stars and creatures, as well as maintaining or changing environments within a region, is created and developed on this dimension.

Sixth-dimensional beings typically act as counselors and guides in society, and often have healing qualities. Fifth-dimensional beings typically work as judges and in law enforcement, but in less political positions than the eighth- or ninth-dimensional beings. Fourth-dimensional beings have expertise in actual production and construction work—typically doing actual construction, participating in energy work in creating a star or planet, or doing whatever else is needed in the universe. The beings of the third dimension and lower can be described as actual material for creations made, working as atomic factors.

The above is a very rough description of what each dimension does, and there are no strict rules about what every being has to do. However, despite the existing hierarchy in the universe and the different roles of the various dimensions, every being was created with a purpose and a need, and there is no concept of being superior or inferior within that hierarchy or in those roles. From the viewpoint of the beings of the Origin, every being from every dimension is a precious part of the Origin. The Origin feels internal harmony only when every being plays its own part properly.

Higher-dimensional beings, including those of the tenth dimension, can, if necessary, appear as individuals, such as humans, which they often do through a duplication process. For example, the first consciousness of the universe and other beings can be incarnated as humans on the earth. They usually do so by duplicating themselves and sending the duplicate (or Subordinate Self) to the earth. The Higher Self and Subordinate Self are discussed in detail in chapter 7.

The relationship between the beings of the Origin and lower-dimensional beings, or the relationships among beings in different dimensions, can be explained using the example of a human body. Imagine that a being of the tenth dimension is the whole body and that beings of the ninth dimension are single parts of the body: for example, the head and face, trunk, arms, legs, and so on. Visualize beings of the eighth dimension as the eyes, nose, and mouth, or as the lungs, stomach, and intestines.

Imagine beings of the lowest dimension—in other words, the first-dimensional beings—as the cells of the body. All the beings of the ninth dimension or lower are parts of the consciousness of the Origin. In other words, all the beings of the universe originate from one source, and always remain as parts of the Origin. This implies that, as each individual being grows, the consciousness of the Origin grows as well.

Although all the beings of the universe are in fact co-workers and siblings moving in the same direction, there is occasional discord among the cosmic members. Those who have an intimate relationship, such as the ninth-dimensional "face" and the eighth-dimensional "nose," move and operate in absolute unity. However, among those with no direct relationships, such as the eighth-dimensional "nose" and the eighth-dimensional "stomach," there is potential for conflict because each argues that its own role should take priority. Thus, discord and disagreement can occur between galaxies or star clusters, but it is usually resolved by mutual discussion or intervention from a higher-level dimension.

As the level of frequency decreases, the capacity to hold information is reduced, implying that the awareness of connection with the Origin may become weaker for a being in a lower dimension. As a result, the intimacy and feeling of connection toward other beings as well as toward the Origin decreases. For this reason, serious disputes can occur more frequently in the worlds of the lower dimensions than of the higher dimensions. Preventing such discord and collisions in the universe is the main motivation for the Gaia Project. At the completion of the Project, all beings of the universe are expected to progress greatly and any large-scale conflicts or problems are expected to disappear.

Just as is the case in human society, sanctions are applied against beings who violate the rules in the universe.

And although it happens very rarely, when beings disturb the fundamental order of the universe, a severe punishment can be meted out, such as a lowering of their vibrational frequencies.

Outline of the Gaia Project

All the beings in the universe have been playing their roles, acquiring experiences in infinite diversity and harmony. However, among some beings, the intimacy toward the Origin and other beings—which is the string that ties all the cosmic members together—has not been strong. Due to this problem, there has been a considerable increase in negative activities among beings, especially in this galaxy to which the earth belongs.

In order to decrease the negativity and increase the connectivity of individual beings to the Origin, an unprecedented large-scale plan was conceived by the first consciousness of the universe. According to this plan, a special planet with distinct energy was first of all created. After a long maturing process of the energy, which will reduce the negativity and enhance the level of consciousness for all beings, the completed special energy will be spread to all the stars in this galaxy and to other galaxies as well. This plan is the so-called Gaia Project discussed in this book.

The Gaia Project is directly related to the earth, which has been at center stage of the Project all along. After the Project was first conceived by the first consciousness about thirty billion years ago, the administrators of the galaxy were consulted.

The administrative center for the Project was established on one of the stars, Sirius, about twenty-one billion years ago, and this center hosted many beings, including the first consciousness, the top administrators of this galaxy, and other high-dimensional beings. About seventeen billion years ago, a holy being for the Gaia Project, which later became the earth's energy itself, was created by the being of the Origin. After determining the best location for the planet, the earth was created about ten billion years ago, with the holy being in its present location.

Following the earth's creation, and during a long period of nurturing of the earth, no visitors were allowed, in order to preserve the purity of the earth's energy. Through the efforts and care of the members of the Gaia Project, the earth's energy matured, blossomed, and slowly spread to cover the earth in its entirety. However, in order for the matured energy to spread effectively and soak into every star and resident being in this galaxy, a special ingredient or "vaccine," which would customize the earth's energy to fit each star, had to be produced.

In order to produce this vaccine, it was necessary to gather all the representative beings from the galaxy. For this reason, all the beings who were attracted to the earth for one reason or another were permitted residency or visitation there, and the earth became a unique learning center in the universe. This opening up of the earth occurred about a million years ago. Since then, the earth has been operating as a place of learning, where beings grow through multiple cycles of experiences.

Now, a million years after the opening up of the earth, the vaccine production process has been completed. It is time to reap the special energy expanding the consciousness of all beings in this galaxy and beyond, which can be done by combining the vaccine with the earth's original energy. Before this completion process starts, however, the entire earth—including the energy world as well as the material world—needs to be cleansed and purified. The completed special energy will then be spread to stars all over the galaxy by the Gaia Project missionaries. With this, the unprecedented project that has lasted for thirty billion years since its inception, and ten billion years since the earth's creation, will finally come to an end.

As the Project ends, the earth will cease its current role as a special place for learning, and it will be born again as a new planet. As the purification process begins, the earth is rapidly entering a stage of turmoil. Details of this change are explained in the next chapter.

CHAPTER TWO
The Great Change of the Earth

It has been a long time since the message of a great change or a great catastrophe on the earth was first delivered to humankind in a variety of ways. The message has been passed down all over the world through legends or folk tales of unknown origin, and also through the scriptures of worldwide religions, which include information about a new utopia, or of final judgment for humankind.

Maitreya Sutra, the scriptures of the Buddha of the Future, tells of a great catastrophe, degeneration, and extinction of the Buddha-law period, which is the period before the opening of the *Maitreya* realm. The Revelation of Saint John the Divine describes God's judgment on humanity at the end of the world. In the sixteenth century, Nostradamus, who is regarded as one of the greatest prophets in human history, predicted that the end of the earth would come at the end of the twentieth century. Edgar Cayce, who is known as the greatest prophet of the twentieth century, also predicted a final catastrophe of the earth. In Korea, Gyeokam Nam Sagoh, Ilboo Kim Hang, and Jeungsan Gang Il Soon also predicted a catastrophe in the near future and the arrival of workers with sacred missions.

During the latter half of the twentieth century, many channelers who can communicate with beings in the invisible world appeared all over the planet, delivering messages of the impending great catastrophe of the earth and its importance for the rise of human consciousness. A relatively large number of people began to experience the opening up of their spiritual senses, some of whom received and are still receiving messages from diverse sources. Their common message can be summarized as follows: *Due to the endlessly destructive behaviors of mankind, the earth has been moaning in agony, and if such behavior is not stopped right away, a great catastrophe will be inevitable.*

Additionally, the earth itself has begun to show warning signs to its residents. Some people have started to feel something unusual in the earth's environment. Volcanoes in many regions have become more active, and earthquakes have occurred more often and on a larger scale than before. Scientists tell us that the ozone layer of the earth changes greatly every year, and that the speed with which icebergs in the Antarctic and Arctic regions are melting is increasing. The climate of the earth clearly seems to be at variance with its regular patterns. For example, a severe weather change, such as a snowy day followed by a hot day, is occurring in many regions, including desert areas of the Middle East, as well as in places like London.

In some countries, such as Korea, people are dazed by the fact that spring flowers, including pear flowers, have started to bloom at the beginning of winter. And flowers such as ume flowers, azaleas, and cherry blossoms, which usually bloom in turn at different times, are now all blossoming simultaneously. This kind of confusion in the plant kingdom was very rare in the past, but it now appears to be repeated in many countries every year.

From the beginning of the year 2005, many people have seen just with their eyes that the sun is emanating beautiful aurora in all directions, although scientists have not confirmed it yet. Some people are also sensing a change in the moon. Either because of their awakening senses or due to the many messages being delivered to humans, more and more people in the world are beginning to know that some kind of huge change is underway on the earth.

However, an absolute majority of people still do not sense any change at all, and in fact this majority refuses to think about such a cheerless possibility as the Great Change on the earth. Instead, people like to argue that the recent and frequent crust movements and unusual weather changes have been happening from time to time in the past, and that these changes can even be dealt with more effectively than before due to brilliant scientific and technological advances.

However, people will have plenty of opportunities to realize the progress of the earth's Great Change and to understand the true meaning of the change either through this book or in other ways. Of course, whether or not a person accepts the message of the Great Change depends entirely on the individual, but if people open their minds to such a possibility, they will perceive, as time passes, the truthfulness of the message.

To be precise, the changes of the earth described in this chapter are not really a description of the future, but rather they are the plan of the Gaia Project. The universe is not operated one hundred percent mechanically, so there can be deviations from the Project. No matter how well-planned it was in advance, there is a slight chance to move away from the plan, since the universe proceeds as a result of the members' collective minds and deeds. On the other hand, a huge universal plan such as the Gaia Project is thoroughly prepared and carried out from the overall outline to the smallest details.

From the viewpoint of the entire universe, there are some beings who are dissatisfied with or even oppose the Gaia Project, and there has been maneuvering going on by such beings to interrupt the plan. Besides, as discussed in chapter 7, the thought forms that will completely disappear due to the purification process of the earth are also, at this point, confusing and disturbing people. But there is no chance that the results will be different from the original plan at all, since the plan was initially made by the first consciousness, and many higher-dimensional beings have been working directly or indirectly for the plan for a very long time. As such, there isn't any possibility of a sudden change in the plan. In this respect, what is written here about the Great Change can be considered to be a description of the future.

This book provides important information about the earth's Great Change, but it does not give detailed facts about its progression. That is because neither I nor anyone else knows all of the details at this moment, and also because, even if the facts were available, no one on the earth would really need such detailed information. Most people will be curious about when and where volcanic explosions, submersions of land masses, weather disasters, wars, and the spread of mysterious diseases will take place because they would like to prepare for those catastrophes. But, as is discussed later, all the individual plans related to the earth's Great Change were already made by each being before this life began. So, at this point, no one can change the plan and there is no reason to do so.

Two Steps of the Earth's Great Change

As discussed in chapter 1, the Gaia Project is a massive-scale project of the whole universe, and it has been in progress for much more than ten billion years. The Project can be divided into five different stages for convenience of discussion:

First, a plan for developing special energy to bring a leap in consciousness to this galaxy was conceived, and the administrative center for supporting the Project was established on Sirius. Second, a special planet, the earth, was created for the Project. Third, the unique energy of the earth was allowed to mature for ten billion years. Fourth, the earth was opened to the whole universe one million years ago, and all kinds of beings were invited to the earth to stay all together. The presence of these beings was necessary to produce the "vaccine" energy. Fifth, after the purification process of the earth is completed, the original earth energy, compounded with the vaccine energy, will be ready to be spread to the entire galaxy and beyond. The earth's Great Change, which is under way now and is related to the fifth and final stage of Gaia Project, is a fundamental and gigantic change in the earth. The Project includes the complete purification of the earth and its ascension to the fifth dimension.

The Great Change can also be divided into two distinct steps. The first step is a complete purification of the entire earth. From the beginning of Lemuria (discussed in chapter 4), the earth has been open to the universe and has been operated as a special place of learning for all the beings who have come to the earth. Inviting diverse beings with different frequencies and different characteristics to the earth was absolutely necessary in order to produce the vaccine energy.

To all the beings on the earth, staying all together for a long period has provided very powerful and unique learning experiences, which could not have been gained on any other star in the universe. On the other hand, various thought forms and negative emotional energy created by human minds during this period have severely contaminated the earth to an unbearable level. Therefore, as the first step of the earth's Great Change, it is necessary to cleanse and thoroughly purify the earth and its residents. This step is essential for spreading the earth's energy to the entire galaxy.

This purification process already began at full throttle from the beginning of 2005, and it will gradually accelerate with various shocking phenomena, including unimaginable crust movements, unusual weather changes, wars, social chaos, and mysterious diseases. The process will end when the axis of the earth is exactly in an upright position at the end of the year 2009. At that time, the material world we see now will be completely destroyed, and the invisible world including the spiritual world in the fourth dimension, as well as several underground worlds, will no longer exist. Only beings who can adjust themselves to the fifth-dimensional frequencies will stay on the earth, with all the other beings moving to stars suitable for their frequencies.

Readers may wonder how the ongoing purification process is different from the previous great events in human history, such as the submersions of Lemuria and Atlantis (see chapter 4.) A clear distinction exists in the intensity of the changes. The previous great catastrophes, which had not been included in the original plan for the Gaia Project, were to restart the materialized human world all over again by sending the people of Lemuria and Atlantis back to the spiritual world. On the other hand, the current purification operation was planned from the beginning of the Project, and it will completely close the earth, which has served as a place of learning during the last million years. The purification process is not simply to stop the physical lives of the beings on the material earth, but it was carefully designed to maximize the growth of each individual's consciousness during the period.

Therefore, the earth's Great Change will not come in the manner of a sudden disappearance of a huge continent or empire in one morning as was the case for Lemuria and Atlantis. Rather, gradual changes of different scales will be phased in and become stronger and stronger over a certain period of time. It is especially important to realize that the earth's Great Change is neither an accident nor a form of punishment from the universe, but rather that it offers the opportunity for people to awaken and expand their consciousness. For example, when people begin to suffer from a mysterious disease, they will realize how helpless modern medicine, in which humanity has so much faith, really is.

The second step of the Great Change involves spreading the completed earth energy to the entire galactic system and raising the frequency of the earth to the fifth dimension, which will completely change the earth's characteristics. While the outline of the earth's Great Change, including the purification process, was planned at the very beginning of the Gaia Project, the ascension of the earth to the fifth dimension was decided at the time of materialization: in other words, around three hundred thousand years ago.

In recent years, the frequency of vibration of the earth has risen gradually and its rise will accelerate for the next few years. Although the ascension of the earth will be completed through various processes over a long period of time, the earth's frequency will reach the level of the fifth-dimensional domain during the second step of the Great Change, from 2010 to 2012. The material earth will begin to disappear and it will become instead an etheric state, as it was during the mid-Lemurian period. At this time, as was the case in Lemuria, all the beings remaining on the earth will once again be able to control their etheric bodies using their minds, and direct communication from mind to mind—telepathy, in other words—will replace the current cumbersome and inaccurate method of communication, speaking through the mouth. In addition, the earth itself will begin its long journey toward the star Sirius, slowly moving away from the current orbit of the sun. But this process will take a long time to be completed.

The decision to raise the earth's frequency to the fifth dimension has a very significant meaning to all the beings on the earth. For those beings whose original frequencies are in the fifth dimension or whose frequencies are supposed to be raised to the fifth dimension due to sufficient learning accumulated so far, there will be a choice to either stay on the new earth or to move to other fifth-dimensional stars. All the other beings whose frequencies are not suitable for the new earth will have to leave the earth. That is, all beings who have not yet reached fifth-dimensional frequencies—regardless of whether they are humans, animals, or plants—will have to leave the earth for a new world.

Since this decision regarding its fundamental change was made, the earth has been operated as a place for learning and has provided various learning opportunities for its residents. In fact, the earth has been a planet where one could experience a growth in consciousness more quickly than anywhere else in the universe. As discussed in later chapters, due to the five sensory organs of the human physical body, as well as the unique earth energy, very vivid experiences have been possible for all the beings staying on the earth. These experiences on the material earth are much more powerful than the experiences offered in other places in the universe, and thus leave much stronger memories. Besides that, the earth has been a place where it has been possible to experience very diverse systems, ideas, and cultures of the universe all in one place because there are all kinds of beings on the earth who came from numerous stars in the universe.

The earth will be changed into a completely new planet and start its new history by the end of 2012. The earth's old face, spotted with violence and war, will be cast off, and will be reborn as a new planet seeking love, peace, and harmony. Earth has been special in terms of its functions as well as its way of operation until now, but it will become a typical, ordinary planet in the fifth dimension. However, to all the beings who have lived here and who will be spread out to numerous stars and planets throughout the universe, the earth will always be remembered as a very special planet.

The Meaning of the Earth's Purification

So far, the earth has been operated as a special training ground for self-learning through experiences. All sorts of beings from the universe have been accepted as trainees, and these trainees have discharged all manner of impure emotional energy generated in the process of their experiences. The earth has silently accepted and purified this exhaled energy from all of these beings. However, whenever the volume of the contamination exceeds its purification capacity, it is inevitable that the earth will have to purify its own energy in unusual ways, such as by trembling, shaking, or twisting its body, or through burping. Such a purification process is necessary because the earth itself is also an energy body.

To get a clear picture of the earth's purification process, imagine the human body. When certain toxic materials are ingested into the body, the body can break them down and neutralize them up to a certain level. But when the toxicity exceeds a certain point, the body has to expel the toxic materials in unusual ways in order to rebalance itself and maintain its normal functions. When the body becomes fatigued due to overexertion, it sometimes develops flu-like symptoms so it can recover.

As a different example, in the case of a spiritual healer who heals people from physical or spiritual pain, impure energy from the patient enters and builds up inside the healer's body during the process of counseling and treatment. The accumulated impure energy closes *hyeols* (acupuncture points) and chakras, gives the healer a stifling feeling in the chest, or makes the healer's entire body utterly exhausted, if the case is serious. In such cases, the healer can recover either by resting for a while or by purifying the body energy through some kind of special practice. This same situation has been repeated by the earth.

As the energy pollution caused by humans becomes too much for the earth to purify by itself, the earth's overall energy changes from a stable state to a very unstable state. Such instability of energy appears on the surface of the earth in various forms of natural disasters such as crust movements and weather calamities, for example, which cause a sudden decrease or temporary extermination of the population of the material earth. Since the beginning of the period of Lemuria a million years ago, small-scale purification works have constantly taken place in different regions, and a few large-scale purifications have taken place as well.

The largest causes of contamination of the earth are various types of emotional energy and thought forms created by the minds of people with negative consciousnesses. Envy, jealousy, anger, and hatred are all the creation of the egoistic human mind. All of these emotions are energy of low frequency, and they pollute every place they stay and whatever they touch. Moreover, every thought is energy, which spreads out in all directions. Thought forms created by strong conceptions of the human mind become living and active energy that then greatly influence people with similar thoughts. (For more about thought forms, see chapter 7.)

These thought forms know very well that they will be isolated from people and that they will become extinct during the earth's purification process. They are now very frightened and are making great efforts to interfere with and postpone the progress of the Gaia Project. They are principally taking advantage of people's gradually deepening anxiety and impatience, which is partly caused by the serious physical changes of the earth. These thought forms sometimes appear in the dreams or meditations of spiritual devotees, as various figures giving some sort of revelation. To create confusion in various places on the earth, thought forms try to stir up the people who can be easily tempted by false messages. That is, they stir up people who have strong egoism and some spiritual abilities, such as an ability to channel, and convince them to ask their followers to consider them to be someone like Christ, the Messiah or Maitreya, or the Buddha of the future.

However, people who are provoking social chaos at the instigation of thought forms are also playing planned parts in the earth's Great Change. Their behavior was expected a long time ago. There are numerous thought forms that are active now, and their tricks are quite artful and intellectual. But there is no possibility whatsoever that these thought forms or the people who are influenced by them can cause any interruption or postponement in the progress of the earth's Great Change.

Unlike the past purifications of the earth, the present purification process is not only purifying all contaminated energy, but it is also moving all kinds of beings away from the earth entirely. In other words, the main operations of this purification process are to nullify all the countless thought forms, to cleanse all the emotional energy accumulated in the human energy body, to get rid of all negative energy that has infiltrated the material world as well as the energy world, and to relocate all beings with frequencies lower than the fifth dimension to other suitable places in the universe.

The multifaceted preparations for the purification of the earth have been going on for a very long time, but the process of shutting down the spiritual world started at the beginning of the year 2005. Until the spiritual world shut down, all beings who were reincarnated on the material earth, including humans, went there after their physical deaths. But it is no longer possible to enter the spiritual world, which has been a place to rest and at the same time a place for all beings to prepare for their next life on the earth. Now, these beings are moving instead to one of the space vehicles in the sky and are leaving the earth for a star or planet of their choice. Currently, there are numerous small space vehicles standing by in the sky to transport these beings to stars and planets with suitable frequencies.

The shutdown of the spiritual world at this time does not yet signify the complete disappearance of the fourth-dimensional world. In the spiritual world, there are still many souls waiting for reincarnation on the material earth so that they can experience the final time of the earth's Great Change. There are also some souls remaining there, until they move to other worlds, without any further plans for reincarnation. The shutdown of the spiritual world means that the earth, which has been operated as a center of learning for so long, has begun to close. It also means that the system of reincarnation is about to end, and that the karma system no longer exists. In short, the earth, as people have known it, is now disappearing.

CHAPTER THREE
Gaia Project Guides

People sometimes imagine heaven or the stellar world, but what each person imagines varies considerably, depending on the individual's knowledge and religious inclination. However, these impressions of heaven do have one thing in common: the imagined place is fundamentally different from current human society.

In heaven, people expect that they will not have to do anything and that everything they need will be provided, with the utmost joy and with ever-flowing peace. In their imaginations, even ascetic devotees who understand the invisible world better may think the same way as most people.

If you have a good understanding of the power of the human mind, you may think that there should be a beautiful place outside the material world where everything can be controlled by your mind. You may even believe that the mind can make anything possible, not only in the energy world, but in this material world as well.

If these people had a chance to remember their past lives outside the earth, perhaps through past-life regression, they may find something very surprising and quite disappointing at the same time. Last summer, during a past-life regression I conducted, one person vividly saw the Gaia Project administrative center located on Sirius and found herself in one of the meeting rooms inside the buildings. She was quite surprised by the dignified appearance of glittering twin skyscrapers. At the same time, she was very much embarrassed by her own appearance, as she was busily moving around and saying, "I'm busy! I'm in a hurry!" She had never imagined that beings in a high-dimensional place such as Sirius would still have to hurry to do their work and deal with tension and stress just as people on the earth do.

It is possible to imagine that, in some place other than on the earth, everything is done automatically or mechanically, and that beings are not obliged to do anything. However, the universe can be harmonious only when all beings are playing their roles or doing their work. The system of the unfolded universe, which was originally conceived and created by the first consciousness of the universe, has been maintained and operated by the collective will of all the beings in the universe—in other words, the will of the Origin. Even the existence of a wildflower blooming in a field is possible only because there is a system allowing the phenomenon and the energy supporting the life form.

Quite surprisingly to people who are interested in the world outside the earth, there are many similarities between the method of operation of the material earth and that of other worlds. Yet this similarity can be explained without much difficulty.

As discussed in later chapters, each person in a physical body has a massive volume of memories, and these memories can be remembered as feelings or as inspirations in everyday life. That is, when people imagine something or when some fresh new idea pops into their minds, what is actually occurring is that something stored in their memories is being accessed. Since human beings on the earth came from numerous stars or planets in the universe, from time to time they are remembering certain mechanisms, systems, and forms they were already familiar with before coming to earth. Thus, when people are inspired to invent, to discover, or to create something very new, a remembrance of the past may occur, and as we know, the earth's civilization has progressed through many big discoveries and inventions.

For instance, most of the diverse appearances of humans, animals, and plants are actually copies of original forms that exist somewhere else in the universe. An interesting example is that of the fashion designer in Korea, internationally famous for his unique designs, who is actually copying the clothes on the star Orion, where he stayed long before coming to earth. It can be said that the present earth is a miniature of the universe. Thus, the common features across nations on the earth may also be very common throughout the universe, while special characteristics in certain regions or in certain ethnic groups may come from a direct transplantation of civilization or culture of certain stars in the universe.

Since the Gaia Project has progressed on a large scale for a very long time, many beings are directly or indirectly involved in the Project. These beings, sent to earth for various missions related to the Gaia Project, are called "Guides" in this book. This chapter explains these Guides in detail.

Firefighters for the Earth

The Gaia Project is an unprecedented plan even in the unlimited universe. It was first conceived by the consciousness of the Origin to accelerate the growth of the consciousness of the whole universe. Along with the holy being created for the Project, energy experts were selected in order to execute the Project, and a very special planet—in other words, the earth—was born in its current location. Since then, those energy experts have been involved in maturing the earth energy and producing the "vaccine" energy.

Around the time that the earth was supposed to open to the whole universe, the administrative center on Sirius began to choose a large number of Guides to be sent to the earth. Higher-dimensional beings who were reliable professionals with a strong sense of duty were selected from throughout the whole universe. As a result, an advance party of Guides was formed.

Their mission was primarily to reside on the earth until the end of the Gaia Project, in order to assist with the final process of completing the earth energy, and to spread the completed energy to the entire galaxy. While awaiting and preparing for their own missions at the time of the earth's Great Change, they have been working as firefighters for the earth. For instance, whenever certain roles needed to be played in order to keep the material earth as an effective learning center, these Guides were reincarnated in physical bodies and they tried to change human society or redirect the stream of human history.

In order to receive orientations about their missions on the earth, the importance of the Project, and the difficulties and pains expected from life on the earth, the Guides gathered on Sirius and in the Pleiades before coming to the earth. Some Guides felt somewhat uneasy about the unknown events they were about to experience, but most of them were proud to be chosen and were excited about the long trip to a new world with many fellow Guides. When the time came about one million years ago, they departed for the earth and they soon joined the others, who had been there for the last ten billion years while nurturing the earth energy. This was the very opening moment of Lemuria, the first civilization on the earth. The leader of this mission was a being called Mu (or Mooh), the consciousness of Origin in the tenth dimension who had originally conceived of the Gaia Project.

When the earth received this advance party, the planet was perfectly pure in its etheric state, and everything was crystal clear. The Guides spent every day in joy and in deep fellowship with others, controlling their bodies as they wished. They established a spiritual society with perfect harmony, centered around Mu.

As time passed, however, beings with relatively low frequencies came to earth collectively, and some of them had negative consciousnesses with strong memories of violence, war, and hatred. As more time passed, the number of such incoming beings rapidly increased. If such a situation had been left uncontrolled, it was expected that the pure beings who came to earth at the beginning of Lemuria would be in serious pain. Unlike the human body of today, those beings with etheric bodies received all the waves around them and experienced unbearable pain from direct exposure to negative energy.

Expecting such circumstances, the Project conceived a plan to materialize the etheric earth. Along with the material world, the spiritual world was set up for beings after their physical deaths, and the system of reincarnation began. (For a more detailed explanation of materialization, see chapters 4, 5, and 6.)

But for the beings with pure energy, life on the material earth was still expected to be very difficult. For that reason, the beings who came to the earth at the beginning of the Lemurian period, including the advance party of Guides, considered going back to their previous worlds. While many beings without missions decided to leave the earth, almost all of the Guides opted to stay until their missions were completed—that is, until the end of the earth's Great Change.

After seeing off many close friends who had been together for a long time, the Guides began to live new lives on the new earth. But life on the materialized earth was excessively hard for them. Living together with beings of negative consciousness was difficult, and living trapped inside an awkward, cumbersome, shell-like physical human body, with no memory of their own previous existences and the purpose of life, was even more difficult.

The Guides were reincarnated on the material earth to guide the earth in the right direction or to accumulate necessary experiences for their missions during the earth's Great Change. Their lives on the materialized earth were usually very painful for them. Like all the other beings, they needed to follow the basic rules of reincarnation, experiencing serious pain in the process. When the Guides were not in the material world, they played various professional roles such as those related to administration of earth, or they acted as counselors and planned for other beings' next lives.

In addition to the advance party, additional Guides were sent to the earth from time to time, particularly during the periods of Lemuria and Atlantis. Most of the Guides have been staying here for hundreds of thousands of years at least, although there are some Guides who were sent to the earth only one or two thousand years ago or even more recently. When new Guides were sent to the earth, it was common for them to stay first in the spiritual world and then to enter the material earth through the physical birth process at an appropriate time.

Among the Guides who were sent most recently, however, there are some cases in which Guides came to the material earth through a special process, called a "walk-in." This process does not follow the usual reincarnation process and is more like a replacement. In the case of a walk-in, a soul leaves a body after its occupant goes through a serious disease or for other reasons, and another being enters the body to live in it. In this case, the new being —the walk-in—may have a difficult time adjusting to human life, especially when he or she does not have any past-life memories of the earth at all. On the other hand, no memory of the earth may be helpful for the walk-in, in order to get rid of earthly notions and recover the original consciousness.

Guides for the Earth's Great Change

Numerous events are happening on the earth now related to the earth's Great Change, and there are many beings on missions who have been working diligently to help make the Great Change happen. While the Guides who have been reincarnated with physical bodies have been mostly in an awakening process, the Guides in energy bodies, called *shin-myeongs* in Korean, have been working hard for the Project. There are still other Guides who work in various space vehicles in the sky over the earth. Because the earth's Great Change is taking place not only in the material world but also simultaneously in the fourth-dimensional spiritual world, there are also many Guides working in the fourth dimension. All of the beings who work for the Project could be called Guides, but in this book the term "Guides" is reserved mainly for those beings with physical human bodies.

Most of these Guides with physical bodies, who have been repeatedly reincarnated on the material earth, are going through an awakening process—in other words, a process of realizing their own existence and their missions. Since their primary missions are related to the final stage of the Project, they have been preparing and waiting—while repeating the round trip many times between the spiritual world and the material world—for their main jobs to begin. In this life, these Guides were all reincarnated in prearranged regions. A large number of these Guides were collectively born in one country and the rest are spread out all over the world.

Because of their strong memories of the universe and the Origin, most of the Guides have been different from other people since their childhoods. Due to their pureness and their inherently high consciousness levels, they feel a strong inclination not to seek the material world but rather to seek something more essential. Since they are interested in the non-material, invisible world, they have looked in on many different religious or spiritual groups for a while, but have never been satisfied with any one group. They often do not get along with the people around them because of their inner feelings about their own existence. And they mostly keep a negative attitude toward authority and order in the physical world because of their inner feelings regarding the origin and order of the universe.

Most of the Guides have not been fully awakened yet, but they are awakening now. Although the awakening can happen as a result of some special practice or meditation, it can also happen through living an ordinary life. The timing of awakening for each individual depends mainly on the time when his or her mission is supposed to start. Once they are fully awakened, the Guides will know who they are and what they have to do, and they will start to do their jobs willingly; the Guides do their missions naturally and willingly without any hesitation. If something is done by force, it is not part of their missions.

These Guides will undertake several types of missions. One group of Guides will work toward people's awakening process, and will help individuals to realize, in various ways, that we are all one and that all beings are from one source, the Origin. But there are many other Guides with other missions as well. For example, when the earth's purification process is over, the Guides representing their own stars will codify the completed earth energy onto their energy bodies and then return to the stars by space vehicles. By spreading the earth energy to their stars, they will help the stars to grow in consciousness.

Other Guides, also traveling in space vehicles, will spread the special earth energy to many stars of which they are in charge. Others will work directly with the space vehicles in the earth's sky. These Guides will carry out their jobs by communicating with the vehicles and providing various types of assistance for their activities in the sky. Some Guides, including beings known as "Indigo Children" or

"Crystal Children," will carry out their missions related to opening up and constructing a new society on the earth.

As mentioned before, the Guides are reincarnated either in one region collectively or else spread out all over the world, depending on the missions they were given. For the Guides who will take the earth's energy to their own stars, each was born and lives in a certain region where the earth energy customized particularly for their stars will be available. When the Guides wake up and become active in their mission, they will each have adequate spiritual ability to complete their given mission. They will awaken at the right time and perceive what their missions are. Even without any special effort, they will begin to recognize one another and form the necessary networks with other Guides.

The *shin-myeongs* from high dimensions are working very busily these days, playing very important roles in the Great Change. Staying in energy bodies, they are carrying out many kinds of missions that cannot be done by the Guides in physical bodies. In particular, many of them are involved in awakening the Guides in physical bodies and preparing them to be ready for their missions at the planned time. Many of the reincarnated Guides are still trapped inside physical bodies and are struggling with lapses of memory, so it is very important for the *shin-myeongs* to awaken the Guides and to get them ready for their jobs at the right time. Many higher-dimensional beings, including the chief administrator of this galaxy and beings known as great holy men in human history, are now, as *shin-myeongs,* participating in the earth's Great Change.

Numerous space vehicles, enough to fill the entire sky above the earth, are now in the sky. Normally, they work in the fourth dimension so that they cannot be seen with human eyes. But when they operate on the three-dimensional earth, they can be detected even by ordinary people. These space vehicles are of various shapes and sizes, depending on where they come from and what they do; they range from small ones for reconnaissance and research purposes to very large ones acting as mother ships.

Although there are also many space vehicles without any mission related to the Project, a large number of space vehicles in the sky now work for the Gaia Project. Until recently, they have mainly stayed in the sky and watched and monitored events occurring on the earth, sometimes engaging in certain activities related to the earth's Great Change. For example, by revealing themselves to some people and by creating the mysterious crop circles, these space vehicles have tried to ensure that the people of the earth know of their existence. The other purpose of their appearances on the earth is to urge people to awaken.

Recently, more space vehicles have come to the sky of the earth from many stars. While many of them have been standing by to transport those beings who will finish their learning on the earth to the stars in the galaxy, they have become more active than before due to the recent closing of the spiritual world of the earth. From the beginning of the year 2005, all of the beings experiencing physical deaths can no longer enter the spiritual world, and must instead go to a space ship in order to leave for a new world. Before boarding the vehicles, such beings have to go through the purification process of "burning" all the emotional energy accumulated on the earth, including karma. During the earth's Great Change, it may be necessary for people in some regions to be evacuated from the earth temporarily. The space vehicles will provide the transportation in these cases, too.

As briefly mentioned before, the Guides will carry out their missions through the manifestation of special spiritual abilities. On the other hand, there are other people with inherently pure energy who have been working or who will work for the Gaia Project in somewhat different ways. They support or assist the earth's Great Change not with special spiritual ability, but rather with their accumulated talent, knowledge, and recognizable social positions in their current lives.

Even before the Great Change began, such people were helping and healing people to open up their spirituality as active spiritual leaders, healers, or internationally known best-selling authors. Though they may not be aware of their roles at all, these people are important for the Gaia Project. Since they do not have special spiritual ability and their activities during the earth's Great Change may not be as prominent as the Guides, they can be called the "Supporters." But the difference between the Guides and the Supporters is only in the way they participate in the earth's Great Change. Such a distinction has nothing to do with their original dimensions or abilities in the universe.

From the very first stage of planning, the Gaia Project has been led by one of the first consciousnesses of the universe—in other words, the third being of the Origin.

A long time ago, the first consciousness sent one of his Subordinate Selves to Sirius to do various supporting jobs for the Project. About one million years ago, when the earth was opened up to the universe for the first time, another Subordinate Self was sent to earth to begin the period of Lemuria. Since then, that particular Subordinate Self, staying mostly in the core of the earth energy, has overseen all the operations related to the Project, as well as the overall direction of the earth. Furthermore, the Subordinate Self of the first consciousness was physically reincarnated into the material earth several times, mainly in order to redirect the stream of human history. This Subordinate Self has now been reincarnated again as a human being, in order to help people expand their consciousness and to ensure that they are firmly connected to the Origin.

PART TWO
THE STORY OF A PLANET

INTRODUCTION TO PART TWO

Presumably, most people have asked the question, "Who am I and why do I exist?" In an attempt to resolve this fundamental question about humankind and to shed some light on themselves, some people have left behind the material world and have lived as spiritual devotees, seekers of truth, or philosophers. Spiritual devotees and truth seekers have made efforts to understand life and the universe by focusing on their intuition and inspiration, practicing in their own various ways, while philosophers have tried to understand the cosmic truth mainly by theorizing and thinking.

However, it seems that such efforts have not brought much success so far. The answers suggested by so-called enlightened people, such as "We are all one," "Everything is emptiness," and "We are all gods," are still not enough to fulfill the seekers' quests. Even the greatest holy men, such as Buddha and Christ, don't seem to have presented a satisfactory explanation of the nature of humanity, nor offered sufficient guidance about how humans should live.

There must be some logical explanations for why their teachings have lacked concrete and convincing answers about human nature. Given the circumstances of the times in which Buddha and Christ lived, periods when people barely ventured away from their homes and no one had a clue what the earth—let alone the universe—was really like, it probably would have been nearly impossible for them to speak about such subjects. And even if circumstances had been different so that such discussions could have occurred, it might have been inappropriate for them to speak in detail about humans and the nature of life, since people on the earth were supposed to grow gradually through new experiences while forgetting about their true selves.

On the other hand, most people on the earth have now been prepared to understand the nature of humankind, what life is about, and the purpose of our being here. Thanks to remarkable scientific progress, most people believe that they have enough understanding of the earth and the universe to receive more concrete answers regarding the fundamental questions of life. Moreover, a great change on the earth is now in progress. The enormous plan known as the Gaia Project has been in process for a very long time, and has now entered its last stage, the earth's Great Change. At this point, every human being needs to know about the real meaning of life as well as the truth about the earth and the universe. Only by such understanding of the Project can we accept the Great Change, which comes to each of us personally as well as to the entire planet, so that we will be able to maximize our spiritual growth during this period.

In the next chapter, I reveal the true history of the earth and human beings and the true nature of all kinds of beings. In fact, almost everything that truth seekers and spiritual devotees have been eager to know about life, existence, and origin is presented there.

CHAPTER FOUR

The History of the Earth and Humans

According to the current, most widely accepted hypothesis of the earth's formation, known as the "low temperature" origin theory, the sun was initially formed by the condensation of the high-temperature gaseous cloud (the solar nebula) in the universe. As the solar nebula cooled down, gas and dust started spinning around the sun like disks. As the gas and dust condensed, planets—including the earth—were formed. The earth was, according to this theory, born at the third place from the sun about four to five billion years ago.

As more materials were condensed by gravity, and the gravitational collapse of radioactive elements generated heat, the temperature of the earth rose. As a result, according to this theory, heavy substances such as nickel and iron sank to the interior and formed the core, while light substances like silicate rose to the surface and formed the earth's crust. Later, volcanic activities released the gases kept inside the earth, which formed the atmosphere. As time went by, the earth cooled down and the water vapor filling the atmosphere changed into rain, creating the oceans. Through this process, the earth's core, crust, oceans, and atmosphere were made almost simultaneously after a billion years or so since the birth of the earth.

As time passed, primitive life forms began to appear in the oceans. This time is called the Proterozoic era. As life forms developed, evolved, and differentiated, some tall plants began to appear a few billion years later, in the Paleozoic era about six hundred million years ago. Very large animals began to appear in the Mesozoic era, starting about two hundred million years ago. Mammals, eventually including human beings, appeared on the earth during the Cenozoic era, which began about sixty-five million years ago.

According to archeologists, the ancestors of humans appeared about five to ten million years ago. They lived in caves and barely survived by hunting animals and gathering fruits and seeds during the Old Stone Age (Paleolithic period) and the Mesolithic period. After those epochs, humans began to make various tools by grinding stones for the first time during the New Stone Age (Neolithic period), which was about six thousand to ten thousand years ago. Next, ancient civilizations—such as Egypt, India, China, and Mesopotamia—began, and they eventually developed into modern civilizations.

However, we should wonder how reliable this geological and historical knowledge is. Any theory explaining the formation of the earth leaves many unanswered questions, and the already established history of humanity is constantly being rewritten. There are so many still-standing ruins from ancient civilizations, such as the Egyptians, the Mayas, and the Incas, that cannot be explained with existing historical knowledge. Even the history of events that supposedly happened a few thousand years ago are often revised significantly whenever new ruins or remains are found, suggesting the possibility that the history we know or accept as fact is fundamentally wrong.

In addition, when people speak about the earth, they only think about the material earth, and when they speak about humans, only life forms with the appearance of human bodies come to mind. Such conceptions can warp the facts greatly. As spiritual seekers and some religionists say, if the human essence is not the human body but non-material spirit or consciousness, then the history of humans is in fact completely different from what we have known until now. Also, if we think of the earth not only as the material earth but also as including the surrounding energy, the formation time of the earth becomes quite different as well.

In sum, the history of humans and the earth presented in this chapter cannot be judged by existing knowledge or mainstream conceptions of "common sense." Rather, it should be judged on its systemicity and the mutual connectivity of the content. Readers may find that, unlike accepted history, the history presented in this chapter will leave no important issues unexplained.

The Rise of Lemuria

While remaining in a pure state of light waves after its formation, the earth was given enough time to nurture its special energy. During this period, with a few exceptional cases, visitors were not permitted. After ten billion years, the earth had thoroughly nurtured its unique energy that would enhance connectivity to the Origin, and the vaccine production process was about to start. To produce the vaccine, it was essential for beings from all different dimensions and layers of frequency to coexist on the earth.

As the earth was initially planning to be open to the whole universe, the beings who would work for the Gaia Project—the Guides—were selected from the entire universe, based on whether or not their specialties were needed to carry out the Project. The members of the advance unit chosen to be sent to the earth gathered on the star Sirius and in the Pleiades for an orientation to the Project and to discuss important issues related to their missions. When the Guides arrived on the earth, they were welcomed by their fellow Guides who had been there for a long time nurturing the earth energy, as well as by their leader—the first consciousness of the universe.

Right before the Guides' arrival, the earth had changed from a state of light to a state of ether. Since the earth had been in a perfect state, devoid of any contamination for the past ten billion years, everything at the time was light, bright, and crystal clear. This was the earth's state when the Guides, alongside other high-dimensional beings with no ties to the Project, arrived on the earth.

During the beginning period, beings with pure consciousness played like children in the entrancing environment. Their bodies of ether were perfectly flexible, and their appearances altered at whim. Feeling genuine fellowship among them, they sang and danced without any worry or dispute. This community was tied together by its central figure, Mu, the first consciousness of the universe. This first society established on the earth was called Lemuria, and its harmony made it a utopian society.

As word spread about the opening of the beautiful earth, more and more beings with diverse frequencies and consciousnesses came for temporary visits or long-term residency. Compared to those who arrived at the beginning, they had relatively lower vibration frequencies and some of them had negative consciousnesses. As the earth's population grew gradually with these new arrivals, negative energy started accumulating, which caused inflexibility in both the earth and its residents' bodies. In other words, due to the increase in contamination levels, the earth's etheric state became less liquid and rather stiff.

After this process continued for another couple of hundred thousand years, the flexibility and freedom enjoyed at the beginning of Lemuria were very much lost. By the halfway mark of Lemuria, when the earth was still in an etheric state, Lemurians lost much of their control over gender and appearance. However, they still maintained their ability to control certain aspects of life with their minds, and the flexibility of their bodies still could not be compared to our physical human bodies now.

The situation drastically changed as Lemuria was approaching its end. The earth was now being bombarded by visitors from all over the universe, and those with lower frequencies and negative consciousnesses arrived on the earth in hordes. So the earth became rigid, and the Lemurian society lost the harmony, joy, and peace that it had so much enjoyed since the beginning. Instead, self-centered egos and disputes among residents arose everywhere. The early arrivals of Lemuria with pure consciousness began to feel pain and fear as they encountered the newcomers, and whenever their etheric bodies were touched by the contaminated energy of the new residents, such pain was amplified. Watching the rapid changes in Lemurian society due to the massive number of new arrivals and their negative waves, the Project headquarters revealed a plan: to materialize the earth.

Materialization of the Earth

From the beginning of Lemuria, many beings with different frequencies of vibration, disposition, and purpose came to the earth. Their energy was essential in creating the vaccine, so that it was necessary to allow all the beings to stay together on the earth until the vaccine reached completion.

However, hardship followed those beings with pure energy as their increasing contact with beings of negative waves caused severe pain. As earth accumulated negativity from the increasing number of visitors, life for the pure beings became hard and miserable. To stop their misery, there needed to be a device to shelter them from negative energy. The answer was to materialize the earth. Unlike on the etheric earth, each being in a materialized world is protected from surrounding energy and waves, mainly because the human body functions as a shield. Of course, this decision to materialize the earth changed the world tremendously.

There was another important reason why the decision was made to materialize the earth. In an etheric state, each being knows basically everything about the other beings, including their original birth information, their past records, and their current energy. In the etheric state, beings tend to avoid contact with those who have negative energy, which prevents the beings from accumulating the large number of experiences they'd get from contacts with diverse types of beings. In the materialized world, where one does not know another's substance, however, such a lack of exposure does not occur. Thus, on the earth, which was being operated as a special school for spiritual growth from experiences, it was decided that a materialized state was preferable to a non-materialized state.

Material is often recognized as the basic element for the third-dimensional world, and the place where humans now live is called the material world of the third dimension. However, the material world is not synonymous with the third-dimensional world. *Gi*, or energy, which is basically waves, is metamorphosed into material or matter by making waves have the nature of particles. Thus, the other dimensional waves, as well as the third-dimensional waves, could be materialized, implying that the matter and materials we see on the earth can also exist in other dimensional worlds (although materialized worlds similar to earth are very scarce in the universe). When the waves of a lower dimension are materialized, matter is more solid and inflexible.

Before the materialization, the etheric earth during Lemuria was in a semi-solid liquid state, which allowed every being to change its appearance to some degree. For that reason, there was no prejudice against other beings' appearances or genders, and every being's true self was conveyed directly through waves. However, as the materialization process began, certain activities or functions possible in the etheric state, including telepathy, were disabled.

Every being of Lemuria was asked to choose from a wide range of life forms: including humans, animals, and plants. If a being chose to live as a human being, it could enjoy immense liberty in exercising its free will and could live like a master of the material earth. Depending on the being's mind and behavior, choosing to live as a human being could be either very beneficial or very harmful to the earth. On the other hand, if a being chose an animal form, its life and its experiences would be limited and sometimes controlled by humans. But most animals, who live instinctively, could maintain their purity and focus on one matter at a time. If it chose a plant form, the being could live a life dedicating itself to other life forms, including humans and animals. Though plants do not have animated lives, they aid others and purify the earth.

During this materialization process, various materialized life forms came on the stage for the first time. It was the birth of what we now call humanity, as well as the beginning of countless plants and animals, each with unique shapes and characteristics. These life forms were generally modeled after creatures already existing somewhere in the universe. From that time on, the earth became an exhibition hall of various creatures collected from all over the universe. After materialization, all beings started experiencing life as humans, animals, or plants, and the earth seemed to provide almost every possible experience available in the universe, only more intensely.

The materialization of the earth did not just mean that every being would now live in an enclosed shell. Due to materialization, every being had to experience the four agonies of life—birth, old age, illness, and death—and all beings were now disconnected, while they lived in the material world, from memories of their previous lives. In addition, the continuity of life ceased as well. Though the beings of Lemuria in their etheric state continued life without interruption so that they did not experience the phenomena of birth and death, this continuity of life became impossible after materialization.

Because of the limited life spans of all materialized life forms, every being on the earth needed to repeat birth and death, and the system of reincarnation was installed. Moreover, it became necessary to establish a world for souls, or a place for beings with no physical form. From that time on, the earth consisted of dual worlds: one the third-dimensional material world and the other the fourth-dimensional, non-material world, which cannot be perceived with the five senses of the physical human body.

Establishing the invisible spiritual world meant more than creating a space for the dead. Of course, the world of spirits offered a resting place for the dead beings who in the materialized world had experienced intense sensations and strong emotions through their five senses. But it also served as an additional place of learning, where their past lives were reviewed and their next lives were prepared.

Since beings with different frequencies could not exist in the same place together, the non-material spiritual world was divided into many sections based on several criteria, including original vibration frequencies and individual preferences. Once the world of spirits had been established, beings after physical death were guided to places suitable for their souls by *shin-myeongs*, or workers of the spiritual world, and stayed there until their next reincarnations. The spiritual world was not only for humans who had died, but also for animals and plants that had died as well. A more detailed discussion of the spiritual world is included in chapter 6.

After materialization, tight controls on entry to and exit from the earth were required to execute the Gaia Project effectively. As mentioned earlier, to spread the earth's energy to each and every star in the galaxy, a special vaccine energy was required. To produce the vaccine effectively, it was desirable to restrict all unnecessary travel between the earth and the other stars and planets. As a result of such a tight control on travel, all types of energy of beings on the earth could be utilized to produce the vaccine. On the other hand, the travel restrictions actually resulted in a general prohibition on leaving the earth until the end of the Project for almost every resident of the earth.

The Collapse of Lemuria

As the materialization process began, the time for a decision came to all the beings of Lemuria, especially the high-dimensional beings who arrived in early Lemuria. One option was to stay on the materialized earth and continue to build experiences or complete their missions by overcoming expected difficulties. The other option was for the beings to give up the original plan and return to the stars from which they came.

The strict regulations on entrance and exit after materialization became a burden for many beings, some of whom disliked being subject to any restrictions. As discussed in chapter 3, during this decision-making period, a large number of high-dimensional beings, who had initially come for the sake of their own experiences, decided to leave the earth. On the other hand, almost all the Guides for the Project decided to stay on the earth until the day their missions were completed.

As the earth became materialized, beings who had been living together in the etheric state of Lemuria were either to be reincarnated on the material earth with various appearances or they were to move to the spiritual world of the fourth dimension. As beings of low frequencies and negative energy continuously arrived on the earth, the overall frequency of the earth decreased, and the materialized human body became progressively more solid. Humans became vulnerable to illnesses, and the span of human life was gradually shortened as well.

The characteristics of the Lemurian society began to change rapidly as material things became first priority for the human beings who were reincarnated. They had no memories of previous lives and had completely forgotten their true selves through the reincarnation process, and so their society had suddenly fallen into material attachment. Though a few Guides who were reincarnated as human beings undertook leading roles in the society, such as becoming priests, it was far beyond their capacity to guide the Lemurians in the right direction. Thus, the materialized Lemurian society fell into a swirl of dispute and struggle, and lost the peace and harmony they once enjoyed. The early culture of Lemuria, in which beings sought spiritual harmony and beauty with the first consciousness of the universe as the central figure, disappeared completely. As people became resentful, jealous, contentious, and were driven mainly by physical pleasure, material greed replaced spiritual joy.

People also created various thought forms by longing for and even worshipping material wealth and power. These thought forms, which will be explained in detail in chapter 7, amplified greed, egotism, and competitiveness within people, and drove the society into a state of confusion, causing serious contamination of the earth's energy. People became anxious to blame others, and even the absolute being, for their unhappiness, sadness, and anguish. As a result, the normal process of learning through experiences almost stopped in Lemurian society. In addition, the emotional energy emitted from the Lemurian people reached a level at which the earth could not purify itself through a normal process. The Project headquarters, which had been monitoring the situation carefully, realized that they could no longer leave Lemuria uninterrupted. They made a decision to give human society an opportunity to start afresh. They decided to stop all the materialistic activities by submerging the continent of Lemuria.

As a result, Lemuria, once the land of dreams that had stretched over the Pacific Ocean, was submerged deep into the ocean in one morning, with only a few islands in the south Pacific remaining above the water. Except for a small number of people who knew of its submersion in advance, the Lemurians shared the fate of the continent. The destruction of Lemuria occurred about two hundred thousand years ago. In a single morning, Lemuria, the very first civilization on the earth, ended its long history.

Hwan-kook and Atlantis

The submersion of Lemuria had an enormous impact on the environment of the earth, causing the earth's crust to move and its climate to change fundamentally. Many new lands arose, including the vast plain stretching over what is now southwestern Asia, central Asia, Mongolia, Manchuria, and the Korean Peninsula, although the human population in these regions was small. On the other hand, the spiritual world was overflowing with beings from the materialized earth. Many beings had to spend extended periods of time in the spiritual world because opportunities to be reincarnated as humans were very limited.

After the continent of Lemuria sank into the Pacific Ocean, the survivors were left wandering in tremendous shock. They were suffering from severe trauma related to the sudden collapse of the land. Watching this situation, the Project headquarters decided to send several high-dimensional beings consecutively as spiritual leaders in order to bring the wandering survivors together and to revive the spiritual civilization of early Lemuria.

The leaders, who were called *Hwan-in*, assembled the reincarnated Guides who were left in confusion with no recollection of their existence and mission, along with other survivors of Lemuria, and established a new spiritual society in the spacious plain of central Asia. Among the seven leaders who would become Hwan-in, the first and second came to earth in the form of light and stayed that way for quite a long time in order to guide people, while the other five Hwan-ins came as humans with physical bodies. This society was later called *Hwan-kook*.

Maintaining the spiritual culture and tradition of early Lemuria, Hwan-kook remained as a community of high spiritual consciousness until an internal discord eventually caused its collapse seven thousand years ago. After its collapse, one of the former leaders of Hwan-kook established a new nation in the northwest region of today's China and kept the spiritual civilization alive. The supreme leader of the nation was called *Hwan-oong*. Then, around forty-five hundred years ago, a group of people branched off from Hwan-oong and established a new nation in today's Manchuria and Korean Peninsula. Their leaders were called *Dan-goon*, who maintained the tradition of spiritual culture from Mu, Hwan-in, and Hwan-oong. In the region of eastern Asia, there are still records of this civilization, and stories of this civilization were passed down among the generations.

Besides Hwan-kook, the spiritual nation in central Asia, people began to establish other new civilizations after the submersion of Lemuria, and the earth's population started to boom once again. During this period, some dwellers of Hwan-kook spread in various directions. Some moved to today's Atlantic region and built a nation that was later called the Atlantis Empire; that was approximately one hundred and fifty thousand years ago.

Because Atlantis was initially erected by the leaders of Hwan-kook, the society succeeded and developed a spiritual civilization at first. With a monistic religious viewpoint, the importance of connecting themselves to the Origin was emphasized, and the society, in a theocratic structure, was led harmoniously by priests who had high levels of consciousness.

However, as the population was rapidly increasing, beings with lower consciousnesses and negative memories reincarnated into the society in large numbers, and this essentially brought Atlantis down from a spiritual society to a materialistic one. Even though the leaders taught others about the invisible world, the consciousness of Origin, and the importance of maintaining a spiritual life, most people lost interest in these teachings and moved further away from spiritual life and thought, giving priority to material things.

Though consistently growing more materialistic, the society of Atlantis went through several serious changes, and its theocratic social structure, with its unity between religion and state, ended during this period. The roles of secular rulers and priests were separated, and priests could no longer be involved in political activities. Scientific technology developed to create material abundance, and egoism drastically increased. As a result, a material civilization prospered while the spiritual growth of humans regressed. New social systems were created based on egoism and competition, and people grew resentful and jealous. They incessantly argued with their neighbors, and riots were a constant occurrence. And because Atlantis advocated a policy of imperialism and enforced obedience, disputes and wars with neighboring nations frequently took place.

Although the conflict within Atlantis was mainly caused by the low level of consciousness among society members, the leadership of Atlantis attempted to solve its social problems by rapidly developing science and technology and by strengthening political authority. Without serious efforts to understand the essence of existence and consciousness, biochemical experiments were thoughtlessly conducted in order to cure all sorts of human diseases, and various fields of science and technology were developed to create material abundance and comfort. As the Atlantis Empire entered its final stage, its material civilization peaked; it greatly surpassed those of surrounding nations, and it even stood far beyond our present civilization.

As their civilization developed rapidly, so did their population. Many beings with low frequencies and negative consciousnesses who did not have opportunities to reincarnate after Lemuria were born again into the society. Many of them were beings who had greatly contributed to the downfall of Lemuria in many ways.

Due to the massive reincarnations of these beings, the spiritual level of Atlantis deteriorated even further, and political power and religious authority were taken over by these combative beings of low frequencies. The general public lost much of their freedom, and ended up living in a strictly regulated society. Numerous thought forms were created by people who worshipped money and power, seriously contaminating the earth energy and driving the society into spiritual rot. When Atlantis hit rock bottom, the majority of people only perceived the material world, and the purpose of their lives was to seek material pleasure. This spiritual downfall of Atlantis pulled down the overall consciousness of the earth and contaminated its energy.

Watching this downfall of spirituality in Atlantis, priests and spiritual leaders sent serious warnings to the people that the downfall would result in a total collapse of the empire. Although they hoped their messages would help to awake the people spiritually, the messages mostly fell on deaf ears and there was nothing to be done for this empire that was already on a severe downward spiral.

So, as had happened in Lemuria, the Atlantis Empire, which had boasted glittering achievements in a material civilization, came to an end. About twelve thousand years ago, Atlantis was submerged into the deep Atlantic Ocean following a series of explosions—explosions that exceeded present-day nuclear blasts in the extent of their destruction.

Here, it is worthwhile to mention two special creatures on the earth: one is the dinosaur, the other the half-man half-beast. Contrary to the common belief that dinosaurs existed and had become extinct long before the caveman entered the earth's history, the dinosaurs actually first appeared on the earth toward the end of Lemuria.

At the Gaia Project administrative center on Sirius, there were serious discussions regarding the state of the earth. The negative energy caused by human minds was increasing, beings of lower consciousness were arriving on the earth in massive numbers, and disputes between conflicting egos were occurring everywhere. In order to lessen these problems, it was decided that dinosaurs, which were a species of another star, would be introduced on the earth.

Although this idea was initially met with protests by several members, who argued that dinosaurs were too dangerous to exist alongside human society, the wild beasts were expected to ensure that people reconsidered their behavior and self-centered philosophy. True enough, the huge dinosaurs crushed humans mercilessly and presented a constant threat to humanity. The appearance of dinosaurs rendered humans powerless in new ways and was therefore an effective method of keeping a lid on the disputes within human society.

However, by the time Atlantis came into full bloom, the culture's civilization and technology were advanced enough to tame the dinosaurs with chemicals and to use the creatures for their own benefit. Even though dinosaurs were far less intelligent than humans, well-tamed dinosaurs were used by people as a means of transportation and in various types of work. Recognizing that the original purpose of sending the dinosaurs to the earth was no longer being achieved, the Gaia Project headquarters decided to exterminate the species completely.

An odd creature that appeared during the Atlantis period was the half-man-and-half-beast. During a time period when most other life forms were sacrificed for human selfishness and biotechnology was very advanced, special experimental creatures were developed in a laboratory in hopes of creating an invincible warrior.

Nature posed various threats to humankind, and especially so when untamed dinosaurs trampled through villages and wrecked homes and families. The people of Atlantis felt that they needed to find a way to protect themselves from such disasters. As a potential answer to this problem, experiments to create various life forms with human intelligence combined with a beast's strength and agility were conducted, but they failed miserably. Instead of invincible warriors, these experiments produced hideous creatures with low intelligence and distorted appearances.

Although the experiments were a total failure, the people of Atlantis found that these creatures were useful as slaves or as third-class citizens, and many half-man-and-half-beasts were created. Before the collapse of Atlantis, some of these creatures spread into various regions, following their masters who migrated into nearby countries. In some areas, like Egypt, there were personal as well as region-wide efforts to heal and convert these creatures into normal humans. Thanks to those efforts as well as to sexual relationships with normal humans, these creatures slowly disappeared as time passed—although their genes still remained in the human body.

After Atlantis

There were a number of people who sensed the end of Atlantis. Before the empire's collapse, they decided to leave their nation and move out toward surrounding nations, carrying their knowledge, technology, and expertise with them. As a result, even though the Atlantis Empire was eliminated from the geographical map and the human population decreased enormously right after the collapse, its civilization spread throughout various regions on the earth. And naturally, as time passed, the overall population of the earth began to increase.

Unlike what had happened with Lemuria and Atlantis, however, instead of one dominant civilization taking control, several civilizations and nations grew up competitively here and there around the world. Among them, there are certain ancient civilizations that still remain utter mysteries. Arising from the regions of Egypt, Central and South America, and the Pacific coasts were civilizations directly transplanted from other parts of the universe. However, when their missions or experiments were accomplished, they returned to their own stars, leaving only some traces of their astounding culture.

After Atlantis, the population growth on the earth raised the energy contamination level once more. Even though higher-dimensional beings reincarnated and remained active as spiritual leaders, their activities were often mocked by people whose addiction to materialism increased over the years. About five thousand years ago, an important decision was made to carry out a large-scale purification project through widespread and massive flooding. These floods affected a large portion of the earth, but especially the regions where spiritual corruption was most serious at the time, including most parts of present-day Europe, and the areas around what are now Israel, northern Russia, and South America. All the material achievements of human-kind in the affected areas were totally swept away by the water, and most areas hit by the Great Floods were turned into desolate wastelands where not only humans but almost any living thing could not exist for quite a while. The small number of survivors of the Great Floods wandered around in great shock until their physical lives ended.

However, as time passed, signs of life peeked through even the most devastated areas. The Great Floods were gradually forgotten, and people started life all over again, with ancient civilizations blossoming in areas where no serious damage had been done by the floods. Memories and stories of the Great Floods were passed down to people's descendents, so that nowadays there exist similar or almost identical legends of the floods in various regions of the world.

After the Great Floods

As had happened many times before, a great portion of the human population on the earth was eliminated after the Great Floods, the spiritual world was crowded, and the opportunity to reincarnate was scarce. Under earth's system of reincarnation, discussed in chapter 6, the next life is planned by taking karma into consideration. Due to this unique system, the opportunity for reincarnation was harshly limited for those who had reincarnated mostly in Atlantis. Along with development of civilizations, however, the population once again increased precipitously, giving the beings in the spiritual world more opportunities to reincarnate as humans again, and made the cycle of reincarnation shorter.

In order to civilize humans spiritually and to purify their minds, some high-dimensional beings of the universe were invited to the earth from time to time. They were born as humans to provide spiritual teachings and to spread various methods of spiritual practice to people. Buddha and Jesus Christ, who are both in the ninth dimension, are the best-known figures in this role.

To the general public who were deeply attached to materialism, Buddha and Jesus described the existence of the invisible world, emphasized the essence of life, and gave some hint of the universe. Their messages often state that happiness is not achieved through wealth or by possessing material goods, but rather through the mind. Jesus emphasized that the "kingdom of God" could only be reached by giving up greed. During the time of the reincarnation of Buddha and Jesus, a considerable number of Guides were also reincarnated. These Guides lived as these teachers' disciples, neighbors, and acquaintances, spreading their spiritual teachings in various ways in order to awaken people's spirituality.

After these great teachers left the material earth, however, the spirituality of humankind once again dropped to almost the same level as before. And the genuine teachings of these holy beings and other spiritual teachers were distorted and falsely reported in sacred books written later. These distortions, which were caused by a lack of understanding on the pupils' part and also by their personal greed, were systematized in the religions that still exist today, some of which are now completely contrary to the wills of the teachers.

As religions became more authoritative in society, the original teachings of the holy beings were lost, or remained only vaguely. Countless religious thought forms were created by the general public, who desired material richness and power, and by religious people who practiced the distorted teachings. These thought forms, initially created by distorted human minds, grew stronger and eventually grasped human consciousness to use humans at their will. By making a pretense of Christ, the Virgin Mary, Buddha, the Goddess of Mercy, and so on, the thought forms, based on the strong desires of the religionists, ironically provided pseudo-spiritual experiences and reigned over those seeking reckless faith. Such thought forms, as well as other thought forms created by idolatry, seduce people and exhaust the human spirit.

After the dawn of the twentieth century, due to industrialization and the sudden explosion of human population, the cycle of reincarnation, which used to be from a few thousand years to a few hundred years in the past, was greatly shortened. The very materialistic beings of Atlantis, who did not have the opportunity to reincarnate after the submergence of their empire, were given the chance to be born on the earth once again.

Human society hurried to be more materialistic owing to these beings' collective reincarnation. Although some people's consciousnesses have expanded with the spread of New Age thought, few individuals genuinely understand the invisible world. Material abundance, followed by the development of science, is serving to increase material attachment. Recently, there have been phenomena such as an increase of religious believers, but this does not necessarily mean that the overall level of the consciousness of human society is increasing. Rather, this increase is a result of people's amplified fear of the future, caused by the astonishingly quick development of material civilization.

Minimum Cosmic Guidance on the Earth

Although the earth is a special planet created for a specific purpose, it has been run as a place of experiential learning since its opening to the universe. For this reason, the earth has allowed any kind of behavior from its residents.

It is true that the overall direction of the material world has been guided to follow the original plan for the Gaia Project. However, under normal circumstances, most of what has happened on the earth has been determined by the collective will of the reincarnated beings, and interventions in the human world from above has been kept to a minimum level. When the earth fell into an extremely undesirable situation where the effectiveness of the learning process stopped, the Guides, who usually stayed in the spiritual world, reincarnated to undertake particular roles to lead the material world in a more desirable direction. Even in such cases, however, since the earth's first priority was to respect the collective will of the beings of the material world, more aggressive interventions were not carried out.

These interventions on the earth have been of one of the following three types: sending spiritual teachers, changing administrative rules, and interrupting history.

Regarding the first type of intervention, when human society in the material world approached an extreme situation with overflowing materialism and egotism causing people to forget their origins, the Project headquarters often let some of the Guides be reincarnated in different regions and work as spiritual teachers or social leaders to lead human history.

Sometimes great teachers from other galaxies, such as Buddha or Christ, were invited to spread spiritual teachings and to straighten out the situations in which people were misguided by the distorted truth of existing religions and beliefs. However, the results were not at all always satisfactory. After the teachers left the physical world, their followers organized new religious groups and have spread new religious conceptions based on their misunderstandings of the teachings of the holy men.

There were also cases in which the administrators of the earth made various changes in administrative rules in order to make people's experiences as effective as possible. For example, the system of karma, discussed in chapter 6, was introduced as a way for all beings on the earth to learn thoroughly and to make each being responsible for its own speech and behavior. Karma is a system in which an individual who offers great charity to others or who generates pain and sorrow in one life will face the opposite situation in the next life. Thus, the system of karma provides a chance to understand other beings well and to become more considerate of them.

However, this system did not work as well as originally expected. People in physical bodies, who knew nothing about the karma system or about the true meaning of life, usually made strong efforts to avoid the pain and sorrow caused by their own karma. It was common for them to blame others or sometimes blame the absolute being while expressing outrage at the world when efforts to avoid pain had failed. Because of such behavior in life, as people reincarnated repeatedly, they tended to generate more karma instead of resolving the karma from their previous lives, thus showing no sign of escaping the vicious karmic cycle.

Unlike the indirect interventions mentioned above, the Project headquarters have also generated some big events that have influenced the direction of human history when human society was heading toward a very worrisome direction, in terms of effective experiential learning. Submerging Lemuria and Atlantis into the deep water or flooding predetermined areas five thousand years ago (the Great Floods) are examples of dramatic interventions by the Project headquarters.

Right before the end of Lemuria and Atlantis, and before the Great Floods, many people lived extremely egocentric and violent lives. Because of the life patterns of these people, the earth energy was greatly contaminated with their extreme emotions, such as resentment, hatred, and sorrow, and people's learning through experiences became limited. This situation did not show any sign of improvement but worsened instead.

Moreover, people were inundated by all sorts of preconceived notions in the name of education as soon as they were born. Many religions, stirring up fear and anxiety, were eager to plant a religious framework in people's minds in the name of a faith or belief. They generated not only many fanatic believers willing to do anything for their beliefs, but also countless thought forms. As the thought forms gained more power because of the increased greed and blind faith people had toward materialism, the earth became more contaminated, and human society fell into even greater chaos. In these circumstances, any meaningful experiences and learning was almost impossible. Even in these situations, to give people an opportunity to avoid a sudden interruption of human history, warning messages were delivered by prophets or spiritual teachers in advance, before a final decision was made.

The earth has been operated as a place for learning through experiences, so the free will of each individual in a physical body has been fully respected. Thus, the material earth has been run by the collective will of people, and the direction of human history has mainly been determined by human beings on the earth. Guidance and interventions into human history from the Project headquarters have been typically subtle and limited.

CHAPTER FIVE
The Human Body

When people speak about the human body, they commonly refer to the skeletal structure, internal organs, circulatory systems, muscles, and other various parts that make up the physical body. It is nearly impossible to imagine that, until the middle of the Lemurian era, beings existed in an etheric state. In an etheric state, a body did not have a fixed form and its appearance and function changed at any time by will. As the earth became materialized during the latter days of Lemuria, the body also underwent a solidifying process, resulting in the physical human body we recognize now.

This materialization did not mean that earth became a materialistic world. Rather, it meant the earth became dualistic, with one world of third-dimensional frequencies and the other of fourth-dimensional frequencies, with many of the third-dimensional waves turning solid. The third-dimensional world of the earth includes both solid materials that can be recognized by the five human senses, and the third-dimensional waves surrounding and supporting these materials. Non-material third dimensional waves cannot be recognized by the five senses.

On the other hand, the fourth dimension of the earth is a world of waves, none of which can be recognized by the human senses. These include not only the spiritual world where beings go after their physical deaths, but also the non-material energy world where the creations of human minds exist and mingle. In the energy world, which can be called a playground of human minds, a person's thoughts or imagination can immediately take shape and form. If a strong thought is repeated over and over, the form grows more distinct and can possibly be developed into thought forms, which become active by themselves.

Due to the coexistence of the two worlds after the earth's materialization, the body of a person is connected to both worlds of different dimensions. Although the human body became much more solid than before, it is still structured to communicate with the waves of the third and fourth dimensions, and even the fifth dimension and above on occasion. In this chapter, I first discuss the meaning of materialization of the human body, and then consider the multidimensional structure of the human body.

The Materialized Human Body

During the last stage of Lemuria, as the earth eventually became materialized, the human body became materialized as well. As will be discussed, there are several important implications of the fact that humans began to live in a material world with materialized bodies.

First of all, the materialization made it much more effective to accomplish growth through experiences. Humans were given five physical senses—sight, hearing, smell, taste, and touch—which intensified experiences far beyond that which was possible with an etheric body. It was also possible to experience strong emotions, especially grief and anguish, through these sensory organs, another impossibility with an etheric body. Due to the severe pains and agonies experienced with their physical bodies, many people came to consider life a continuation of pain. Some even chose to take their own lives when they found the weight of their experiences too heavy to carry. However, despite such difficulties generated by the materialization, intense experiences are stored as powerful memories and serve as effective means of learning.

Secondly, the materialization of the human body created the four agonies of life—birth, illness, old age, and death. The etheric body had the option to stay in the same condition as long as the being desired, due to the immense flexibility it possessed, but the materialized body gradually changes as time passes. Even though the materialized body constantly produces new cells to replace old ones in order to maintain the original form of the body, newly produced cells can be slightly different from the original ones, and sometimes distorted or degenerated cells can be produced. Thus, the function of each organ becomes either weakened or paralyzed as time goes on. Therefore, materialization of the human body inevitably accompanies a process of creation called birth, a deterioration of its function called old age, a dysfunctional state called illness, and a fading away called death.

Until now, the span of human life has been directly related to the state of materialization. Although the human life span has increased due to the rapid progress of medical science in the twentieth century, it had been on a gradual decline through the entire human history on the earth. Unlike the etheric body, which maintains complete flexibility at all times, the physical human body grows old. Parallel to the extent of materialization, the adaptability of the human body to the outside environment has also declined. After Lemuria, the overall frequency level of earth declined, causing the intensity of materialization to increase and the extent of materialization to broaden. These effects led to the human body becoming more solid and consequently losing more of its flexibility, which naturally shortened its life span.

At the beginning stage of materialization, the typical span of human life was over one thousand years, but this drastically decreased to less than a hundred years following the Great Floods five thousand years ago. Such a drastic reduction in the human life span happened all over the world, but not at a uniform rate. For example, the span of human life in Hwan-kook stayed rather steady for a long time, but suddenly decreased when the society was experiencing the downfall of its spiritual civilization about seven thousand years ago.

Thirdly, the materialization of the human body meant disconnection from past-life memories. When human beings are in a physical body, all cognition and thoughts are completed through a materialized organ—in other words, the human brain—so that all memories saved in energy format are discontinued. In other words, from the moment of physical birth, humans are programmed to forget all past memories as long as they're physically alive. Except for special circumstances, people cannot connect with memories before birth. Thus, within the materialized body, one can only perceive himself or herself to be a visible, touchable, living, breathing human body without knowing his or her true self. Even special abilities or knowledge developed over many lifetimes remain only as vague feelings during one's lifetime. Such a lapse of memory about oneself is not a common phenomenon in the universe, but one that is distinct to this material earth.

The lack of past-life memories can be a very important characteristic on the earth, where people are intended to have intense experiences through the five senses and to learn through those experiences. In other words, the loss of memory due to the materialized body is, for a couple of reasons, surely necessary so that people can have effective experiences.

One reason involves spiritual information. In the universe, though not on the materialized earth, every being possesses a perfect spiritual knowledge or spiritual information. Since all beings correctly understand their own existence and their relationship with the origin of the universe and live together with other beings of similar frequencies and characteristics, such openness of spiritual information does not cause any restriction or hindrance to any being's life. Yet in the case of humans on the earth, who live with a sense of discrimination and competition, human relationships would be greatly constrained and humans' experiences would be interfered with if people knew all the spiritual information about themselves and others.

Another reason is that if a person still possessed memories of past lives, new experiences in the present life would be difficult. It's often emphasized in spirituality to focus on the present moment. What prevents this from happening are mostly memories of the past and concerns for the future. When the mind is not focused on each present moment but instead dwells on past memories, events may occur but new experiences do not. If people remembered everything from their past, new experiences would be difficult to attain for this reason. In each life, we have numerous memories, including those we don't necessarily want to remember. Constant recollection of such memories would cause unnecessary pain. From that perspective, memory loss caused by our materialized bodies can help greatly to generate intense experiences on the earth.

For this reason, even though many have sought after truth and desired to know themselves, the true picture of the earth and the universe has been hidden, and the truth about humanity's existence has been obscured. The truth of the universe discovered by "enlightened" people through special experiences or spiritual practices are in fact mere fragments of the whole picture, and the knowledge such people acquire about the universe is likely to be incorrect.

Additionally, the materialization of the human body interrupted the continuity of life, which required the introduction of a reincarnation system. Materialized human beings live with birth and continue to live until physical death. After a certain time period, the human repeats this life and death cycle. Because of the operation of this reincarnation system, it became necessary to have a resting place for beings while they were outside of materialized bodies. The spiritual world was set up for this purpose in the fourth dimension, which cannot be sensed with the five senses of human beings. To those who only accept that which they can directly sense, the system of reincarnation can be difficult to accept, but the materialization of the human body made the cycle of rebirth and the spiritual world necessary.

Finally, after materialized bodies were introduced, lies and hypocrisy became possible. Contrary to the telepathy used for communication in an etheric state, humans in physical bodies have no way to communicate other than by spoken and written language. That is, humans cannot read each other's minds, so numerous tragedies have occurred due to lies floating around human societies.

Although excessive lying became one of the distinguishing characteristics of the materialized world, it also provided an opportunity to learn about truth and honesty. In this respect, the materialized human body has contributed to shaping the earth as an ideal place of learning through experiences.

That beings once existed in etheric bodies can be an eye opener to many people who identify themselves with their physical bodies. To those who recognize life only through their five senses and accept death as the extinction of being, this fact offers a hint of what human nature really is.

As we have seen so far, the physical bodies of humans are merely enclosed disguises, or shells of the whole body. Each of us is inherently a being of consciousness or a spiritual being, and can be shown in a form that is completely different from the appearance of a physical human being. When we wear a disguise with a human form, we are called a human being. When we wear a disguise with the form of a whale, we are called a whale. When we wear a disguise with the form of an alien, we are called an alien. No matter what kind of disguise we wear, however, our nature does not change. There is no difference between a human, a whale, and an alien in terms of nature. In this respect, humans are only beings disguised with the human body.

Multidimensional Structure of the Human Body

The human body after materialization consisted of the material body and the non-material body of the energy state, and these two bodies are connected together through a gate called *kyeong-hyeol*, or chakra. The gates are mostly open during childhood, but are gradually clogged up by negative thoughts and impure energy.

By adulthood, it is common for the gates to be entirely blocked except for a thin passage that can barely maintain the body. When energy does not circulate well, people can only perceive the material world through their five senses—in other words, the materialized sensory organs of their bodies—and therefore can only perceive their physical body. However, people who have opened their *kyeonghyeols* through the practice of *gi*, yoga, or other methods can simultaneously perceive both bodies.

People with open chakras have another sense, commonly referred to as the sixth sense. A few people can see the human aura that surrounds the body, perceive the energy that is wrapped around objects, and sense the subtle movement of energy itself. The halo—the special energy surrounding the heads of saints—was discovered in this manner, and was often depicted in sacred paintings. Human energy, or auras, have not been proven to be a scientific fact, but there is strong evidence suggesting their existence. The concrete form and function of auras have not been properly measured with physical instruments, but they have been described for centuries by meditators and people with special abilities. To give a clear picture of the multidimensional structure of the human body, I will briefly explain what has become known about the human aura and chakras so far. (I also explain this information in my first book, *What We See Is Not the Only Truth*.)

Human energy consists of seven or more layers with different frequencies of vibration. Due to these differences in frequencies, the physical body overlaps different layers of aura in the same space. Each aura layer is different not only in frequency but also in scope, shape, and function. Aura layers of higher frequencies extend farther away from the physical body. For example, the etheric body, which is the first layer, has a shape similar to, and includes the space of, the physical body but extends a little farther beyond the body. In the same manner, the second aura layer includes the space of the first layer and extends a little farther than the first. The layers of the third layer and above exist in the same manner. So the highest aura layer extends the farthest away from the physical body and embraces all of the other aura layers as well as the body.

Each aura layer is related to specific human functions. The first, second, and third layers are related to the functions of the physical body, while the fifth, sixth, and seventh layers are related to spiritual functions. This fact means that the energy of the first, second, and third layers consist of three-dimensional waves supporting the materialized body, while the energy of the fifth, sixth, and seventh layers are of fourth-dimensional waves of the non-material world.

In general, higher frequencies are closer to the Origin of the universe, so the aura layers with higher frequencies are relatively closer to the Origin of the universe than are the aura layers with lower frequencies. In other words, the aura layers with higher frequencies influence the layers with lower frequencies—but it doesn't work the other way around.

The highest aura layer is closest to the Origin of the universe, and the physical body, which has the lowest frequency, is the most peripheral part. That is why illness shows up in the etheric body, which is the first aura layer, before the symptoms appear in the physical body, and it also explains why the illness of the physical body naturally disappears when the aura layer recovers from the abnormality.

The seven layers of aura surrounding the physical body constantly move and are active while connected to the seven chakras that Indian yogis describe. The first chakra is the gate that connects the human body to the first aura layer, the second chakra is the gate that connects the human body to the second aura layer, and so on. When the first, second, and third chakras are thoroughly activated, they mutually connect to the first, second, and third aura layers of the human body so that physical health improves. This connection means that spiritual practices focusing on physical health develop the first, second and third chakras, enhancing the flow of the third-dimensional energy between physical and non-physical bodies and hence improving physical health.

On the other hand, when the fifth, sixth, and seventh chakras are thoroughly activated, they become connected to the spiritual energy of the fourth dimension, so that the person becomes more interested in spirituality. Spiritual practices that mainly focus on spiritual growth develop the fifth, sixth, and seventh chakras, so that the body becomes well connected to fourth-dimensional energy and recovers spiritual health and manifests some spiritual faculties.

The energy layer of the fourth aura, which reflects a person's current state of mind, is connected through the "heart" chakra, or Anahata Chakra—that is, the fourth chakra. It is known to intercede between the third-dimensional frequencies of the first, second, and third aura layers, and the spiritual fourth-dimensional frequencies of the fifth, sixth, and seventh aura layers.

Because control of the heart chakra, including its opening and closing, is operated by the mind, a person can either sublimate the third-dimensional physical energy to the fourth-dimensional spiritual energy or utilize the fourth-dimensional energy for better physical health. When a person encounters physical death, the human energy is reconstructed. The third-dimensional physical energies disperse into the earth, and the rest, the fourth-dimensional energies, are consolidated into a single stream, departing for the spiritual world in the fourth dimension.

It should be noted that the seventh human aura layer stores all the records of a soul's past. Anyone who understands the world of energy knows that everything about this world is recorded and that the records are never erased. Every soul always stores all of its own records inside the energy body. According to Barbara Brennan, who is known internationally as an expert on the human aura, the seventh layer keeps the bands of past-life records, and they can be watched just like a movie. The seventh layer stores not just the circumstances of each moment, but also all emotions related to those circumstances. These records can be deciphered by focusing on the frequency of the seventh layer. Thus, it becomes possible to cure various diseases related to past lives through appropriate methods such as hypnotherapy.

In this manner, the human body is connected to the third-dimensional waves that support the physical body through chakras as well as the fourth-dimensional waves that create non-material thought and generate interest in spirituality. Moreover, the human body is equipped to connect with the earth energy and universal waves of the fifth dimension or higher. Several more chakras exist above the seventh "crown" chakra, or Sahasrara Chakra, which function as a gate to the energy higher than the seventh aura layer. However, energy beyond the seventh layer no longer belongs to any individual's aura, but instead reflects the total consciousness of each dimension. Since most people's consciousness while on the earth does not pass beyond the fourth dimension, the higher-dimensional chakras are not activated, except in some special cases.

Flexibility of the Human Body

Although beings became constrained in stiffer bodies after materialization, the human body is still more flexible than most people believe. Since the energy surrounding humans greatly influences the physical body, and the energy itself can be controlled by the human mind, people can use their physical bodies in flexible ways. There are many examples that demonstrate the extent of the human body's flexibility, and how influential the mind is on the body.

According to biological and medical knowledge, a human can only maintain optimal health with a certain intake of calories and nutrition per day. If someone consumes neither food nor drink, that person can survive no longer than a few days. If someone drinks only water, then that person can survive only for about a month at most. However, there is a known case of a woman who has lived just by drinking water for decades without any health problems, and some Taoists live healthy lives by eating only very small amounts of food.

It is common knowledge that someone who falls into icy water will die within minutes, and that someone who walks on sizzling fire with bare feet will instantly get severe burns. Yet some Indian yogis have demonstrated the ability to survive in icy water for several hours, and to come out unharmed after walking on fire. Some might believe that such examples show the flexibility of the human body only for those who are specifically trained. However, similar examples have been documented that involve ordinary people who have received no special training at all.

Multiple personality disorder (MPD) is a dissociative disorder in which two or more distinctly separate personalities exist in one individual. Whenever a person with MPD changes from one personality to another, brain waves, blood circulation patterns, tension of the muscles, pulse rate, attitudes, and allergy response also change, and even scars or other physical marks appear and disappear, depending on the particular personality. The individual's change from one body to another is instantaneous. Regardless of its cause, MPD is strong evidence for the tremendous flexibility of the human body.

Still, phenomena that demonstrate the flexibility of the human body do not often appear in most people. For instance, some people can live for a long time without eating any food, but long-term fasting would bring death for most others. And a great majority of people would be far from safe when walking on a sizzling flame; instead, they'd be badly burned. Such differences in the flexibility of the human body, as the next chapter explains, are caused by differences in each individual's beliefs or by their accumulated past-life memories. Some people who have realized great flexibility of the material body through long practice over past lives and during this lifetime are not harmed by a lack of food or by walking on sizzling flames. But most people who have strong memories of the limitations of the human body would indeed be badly hurt by trying to imitate the specially trained Taoists or yogis.

Connection with the Mind

Many people seeking truth have contemplated the power of the mind, but have not found satisfactory answers. This is because what we refer to as "the mind" does not have just one function or one generic character but is actually very complex, with various sources and functions. For example, when people say they are happy or sad or simply say "I don't mind," they are describing an emotional state of mind. But when people say "I can't read your mind," they are referring to the deep intentional mind. And when people say "Do what your mind tells you," they mean the will, thoughts, ideas, or desires that come from the mind.

The mind can be controlled by the will or thoughts, but in many cases, the mind is beyond one's control.

Occasionally, a deeply stored memory will rise to the surface and make a person sad or depressed. Sometimes, the mind suddenly changes as a result of thinking or analyzing, a process that can happen unconsciously. In that case, the change is often caused by memories from the past or by outside energy. This outside energy can be the guardian spirits who stay in the aura layers and protect or guide the person from great dangers or from going the wrong way. Outside energy can mean various thought forms created by human minds or souls who weren't able to leave for the spiritual world for some reason. Though some people might be weary of their capricious minds, such changes in state of mind are inevitable and can happen to anyone at any time.

Among several facets of mind, it is "consciousness" that allows a person to do certain things according to his or her subjective will. Consciousness offers the ability to perceive the world and to be creative, and it exercises absolute importance to human life through the heart chakra located in the center of the human body. Aura layers are activated when a person focuses the consciousness on a certain layer, directly influencing what form the person's life takes. The consciousness of an inherently lower frequency is mainly attracted to the material world. Thus, the third-dimensional aura layers frequently become activated by the heart chakra, and the individual consequently grows attached to the material and physical body. The consciousness of a being of inherently higher frequency, however, focuses mostly on the non-material, and thus the fourth-dimensional aura layers become activated and the spiritual life moves into focus.

Consciousness is a tool given to each soul to explore and learn about the world. It enables one either to control or to convert energy, which explains why people either purify or contaminate the fourth-dimensional energy world without noticing the consequences of their actions. Everything the mind visualizes or imagines becomes configured in the energy world. Thought forms are constantly being created, which is a significant cause for the earth's contamination. (Please see chapter 7 for more information about this topic.)

Consciousness also enables one to focus on any frequency, and thus it becomes possible to communicate with any being of any frequency through one's mind. When one receives new information and perceives it clearly, the consciousness allows, by adjusting its frequency, a connection to the energy regarding that new bit of information. For instance, it is not possible to establish an energy connection with plants when an individual misconstrues the plants' state of existence, but from the moment the individual becomes aware of the equal nature of humans and plants, it becomes possible to initiate a connection.

When an individual misinterprets the world or possesses incorrect information about the existence of a certain entity, the consciousness cannot adjust to the correct frequency. Thus, under such circumstances, no amount of effort can lead to a connection. In the same context, as long as people misinterpret the messages of Buddha, Christ, or any other holy being, regardless of how much they pray, there will be no energy connection with such holy beings. It is much more likely that people will become connected with thought forms that they themselves create, and sometimes end up receiving misleading revelations through prayer, meditation, or dreams.

In this manner, consciousness, which controls energy through the heart chakra, directly influences the energy world and the human body as well. The most common example demonstrating the strong influence of consciousness or the mind over the human body is the placebo effect. If an individual believes strongly enough in a placebo's potency, then that placebo—an inert pill or liquid—is able to cure medical problems. Likewise, non-alcoholic beverages can make a person drunk. Imaginary pregnancies can occur in females who eagerly want to become pregnant.

Healing diseases or improving athletic performance through the imagination, also called imagery, is also possible. Such phenomena show that the physical body does not respond to what really exists, but rather to what a person believes to exist. These phenomena occur because consciousness, or the mind, controls human energy through the heart chakra and affects the human body. The mind affects not only the human body, but it also directly affects the material world. Support for the existence of such phenomena can be found in demonstrations of psychokinesis by people with extra-sensory perception (ESP), and from scientific experiments involving dice tossing. The mind of an individual, with great concentration, confidence, and faith, manifests great power.

Some spiritual devotees have exaggerated the power of the mind, insisting that humans can achieve anything through the mind. They say the mind creates everything in the world. However, every human who lives on the earth is a disciple learning through lively experiences, and the mind is just a tool given to each individual for those experiences. This means that the mind is not a tool for material creation, but rather that it is a basic tool for creating experience. This tool can manifest creations only in the third and fourth dimensions of earth.

CHAPTER SIX
The Lives of the Earth People

Unlike most stars and planets in the universe, the earth was formed through a very special process and has been operated for its own distinct purpose. Generally speaking, stars and planets in the universe are relatively simple in their specific functions and characters. The dimension of a star and its laws of function are determined in advance when the star is created, and only beings with vibration frequencies and characteristics suitable to each star are permitted to reside there.

In contrast, the earth was formed to generate and cultivate the special energy that would strengthen connectivity to the Origin. For this purpose, all beings who desired to come and have diverse experiences were accepted as residents of the earth. Thus, the earth, which accommodates many diverse beings from all over the galaxy, has been very unique in many respects, even from a cosmic viewpoint.

As discussed before, after remaining in the state of light waves for a long time since its formation, the earth was opened to the universe in an etheric state about a million years ago. From that time on, the earth has been a place of learning for beings who wanted to experience the earth's energy. Especially since the earth's materialization, human beings have repeated, through a system of reincarnation, the cycle of experiences followed by a period of rest. Humans have been able to have vivid and intense experiences through their five senses on the third-dimensional material earth, and could then take some time off to rest and recharge in the fourth-dimensional spiritual world.

Although the earth offered learning experiences to every being in its atmosphere, humans living on the material earth have lost their sense of identity after losing their memories of their past lives. Many felt stifled and were anxious to find the meaning of their existence; those who had stronger feelings of the universe beyond the earth were more frustrated. A few people who experienced various spiritual phenomena could sense the existence of another world and overcame the fear of death, or the fear of their physical bodies disappearing.

However, spiritual experiences didn't lead people to the correct conclusions about, or to an accurate understanding of, the energy world and the universe. People who vaguely understood the spiritual world and karma often lived while also worrying about the rewards or punishments they thought they might receive in the afterlife. Some people gained a level of understanding of the essence of life through special energy experiences or "enlightenment," but even those "enlightened" people could not perceive the world beyond the earth. They might have believed the world was composed of heaven, the earth, and humans, but their heaven was merely the fourth-dimensional spiritual world of the earth.

This chapter examines the true nature of human beings and life. Although there have been many enlightened beings on the earth, their perceptions had limits and none of them have clearly explained the true meaning of humanity and human life. The reason, of course, is that the earth has been a place for learning through experiences, a process that includes a complete lapse of memory about the past. As mentioned in chapter 5, if people had been able to retain their memories of the meaning of life and were fully aware of their identity during their physical experiences, the effectiveness of learning would have been greatly reduced.

But now it is time for people to wake up from their long lapse of memory and their momentary sleep, in order to reexamine their past and realize who they are. As described in Part Three, the role of the earth as a place of learning is over, and it is time for all residents to wrap up their time on the earth and move on to other places that suit them.

The System of Reincarnation

When the earth began to materialize, the continuity of life came to an end, and people started to be reincarnated over and over. Since then, the earth has played its role strictly as a place of learning, where every being goes back and forth between the third-dimensional material world and the fourth-dimensional spiritual world. By establishing the spiritual world for new arrivals from all over the universe as well as for beings after physical death, the system of reincarnation began to work at full scale.

The spiritual world was a place not only for peaceful rest after the harsh experiences in the material world, but also a place for diverse activities. Until now, people have either known nothing about, or have had very fragmentary knowledge about, the existence of the spiritual world. Some have imagined the place as *Sukh vati*, the abode of perfect bliss, as heaven, or as a paradise where gods and angels live. Other people have pictured a dark and dusky world of ghosts, or a place where the king of hell judges the dead and either rewards or punishes them based on the behavior they engaged in while living on the earth.

Like much information about spirituality, such storybook imagining of the spiritual world is far from the reality. The same can be said of visions during out-of-body experiences or meditation. Usually, those visuals are only part of the vast spiritual world or are part of the world of phantoms created by the human mind.

Roughly speaking, the spiritual world consists of several places with distinct roles: the "place to remember the past life," the "place for complete rest," the "place for activities," the "place for preparing for the next reincarnation," and other places designated for special purposes. All beings—whether they were people, animals, or any other life form—are guided right after physical death to the spiritual world.

The first place that all beings arrive right after physical death is the "place to remember the past life." In this place, with help from counselors working for the spiritual world, each of the arrivals reviews every moment of their past life and has time for remorse—not remorse from any viewpoint of human society but rather from the standpoint of spiritual growth from experiences. After finishing this process, the newcomers to the spiritual world move either to the "place for complete rest" or the "place for activities."

While beings who had extreme experiences in the physical earth may go to the "place of complete rest," the other beings move to the "place of activities," which is vast and consists of many different parts. Based on many considerations—including the type of life form they were in their previous incarnation, their original frequencies, their past experiences, and the next reincarnation plan—each of the newcomers stays in one part of the "place of activities" and mostly remains there until the next reincarnation. Although it is true that most learning for beings on earth results from experiences on the physical earth, some learning also occurs in this spiritual world.

For every being who is supposed to become again a life form on the physical earth, the "place of preparing for the next reincarnation" is the last destination in the spiritual world. In this place, with professional help from a life planner, each being plans his or her own forthcoming life on the material earth.

In the spiritual world, there are many beings taking various roles, who can be called *Shin-myeong*. For example, there are beings who guide the dead from the physical earth to the spiritual world or help beings entering the physical earth. Some beings work as counselors, welcoming the beings back from the material world and helping them review the lives they have just finished, which can make the beings' consciousnesses grow. There are also planners who help souls plan for their next lives.

In addition, there are some beings who work as administrators for the spiritual world. Though they oversee the third- and fourth-dimensional earth and guide the earth in a desirable direction, the way those beings work is quite different from the way they work on other stars. On most stars, all residents partake in discussion and the administrator carries out the decisions. On the earth, however, for the sake of creating a center for learning, indirect and covert control is exercised.

Occasionally, when the material world lost sight of its purpose and people became more and more obsessed with material goods, Guides were sent to the material world to take on active roles as spiritual leaders. Frequently, during the Guides' lifetimes, the world generally moved in a desirable direction, but once the Guides returned to the spiritual world, people often went back to their previous lives of jealousy, resentment, egoism, discord, and hostility. People even organized religions and doctrines claiming to remember the valuable teachings of their spiritual leaders, but doing so only brought greater chaos than before.

The spiritual world, as mentioned before, served as a preparatory school where beings prepared for their next life on the earth. Due to events such as the submersion of Lemuria, the collapse of the Atlantis Empire, and the Great Floods, the population of the earth repeated a pattern of temporary increase followed by a drastic drop. Therefore, most beings spent much more time in the spiritual world than in the physical world, and the opportunity for reincarnation was, in general, rare.

To accommodate such circumstances, a great deal of preparation was made to maximize the learning process while in the physical world. Beings planned their upcoming lives meticulously, and prepared in many ways to achieve an expansion in consciousness. Although the intensity of life in the spiritual world was much less severe than the intensity of life in the material world, beings in the spiritual world could also learn much from their diverse roles or activities. How beings spent their time in the spiritual world was also an important factor in raising their consciousness.

Reincarnation usually happened in groups, which meant that beings who knew each other well through past lives were usually born together in the same region at the same time in order to experience various types of relationships among themselves. Such an experimental group was sometimes formed with advance agreement when beings planned for their next lives, but group reincarnation was usually undergone to resolve karma created in beings' previous lives.

People created different kinds of karma during each lifetime. They were then born again with related souls in order to settle the karmic debts that they had created.

However, during this process, these beings created new karma with beings with whom they had previously had no relationship, and thus it became necessary for them to be born again with those souls because of the new karma. For this reason, it was common for beings to be reincarnated with a group. Such a phenomenon has been called "collective reincarnation" in certain literature.

In general, karma has been perceived as a sort of payback in the next life for any mental or physical damage one might have received from another in a past life, or as a reward in the next life for all the good deeds achieved in this lifetime. Many spiritual devotees have accepted karma as a law of cause and effect, or as the natural consequences of one's deeds and misdeeds. They believe that a life of joy and abundance is caused by good deeds in a past life, and a life of severe pain is caused by misdeeds in a past life. Such symptoms exist, but the essence of karma has been misunderstood.

Karma, in fact, was one important rule of reincarnation that was introduced at the time of the earth's materialization. Contrary to most people's idea of reward and punishment, and running parallel to the concept of heaven and hell, the purpose of the rule of karma was to encourage responsibility for one's speech and behavior and to thoroughly learn from those experiences. If an individual makes another individual suffer pain, receive grief, feel resentment, or even the opposite—feel joy and appreciation—he or she will experience the opposite situation with the same being in another life.

Learning about human relationships can be completed by experiencing the opposite situation as well as the original situation. At first, such karma was restricted to relationships between individual souls, but later its application became broadened. For example, if an individual mistreated animals for no particular reason in one life, the being would be reborn as a mistreated animal in the future reincarnation.

Karma can also be explained from the viewpoint of energy. If a particular energy accumulates from a relationship, the energy will continue to influence not only the original person's life but also the life of the other person in the relationship in many ways until it is resolved. For instance, if an individual lived with immense hatred and anger toward another individual or even toward society, then that individual will accumulate a great deal of negative energy, and naturally the person's mind and behavior will be influenced by that energy. Thus, to recover from the distorted mind and behavior, the bitter and entangled emotional energy of the soul needs to be resolved.

The system of karma helps to release the accumulated energy through mutual relationships. If someone hated another person in one lifetime, that being will resolve such built-up emotional energy by meeting the other being who caused such feelings, experiencing the opposite situation in a different life. If it is not resolved in one lifetime, the situation will be repeated until it is finally resolved.

Many individuals believe that life is controlled by karma and that every deed generates karma, but that is not the case. Occasionally, while planning the next life in the physical world, some beings have taken roles in order to create conditions and circumstances for an entire society to experience immense pain. In this case, though a certain individual actually created the tragedy and hence was responsible for occurrences in the physical world, they were, from the spiritual perspective, only undertaking their missions as planned. In such cases, therefore, the rule of karma is not applied. Although some people speak of the karma of ethnic groups or nations, karma is strictly a rule for learning that applies on an individual level.

In this regard, like actors going on stage, all beings on the earth have been mere students who had rehearsed in advance in the spiritual world, performed in the material world for vivid and diverse experiences, and then came down from the stage into the spiritual world following the rules of reincarnation. It is true that almost everyone complains about the pain of life, but this is merely because people have forgotten their own identities and the reason for existence.

Pain in life can only be reduced or stopped through a clear understanding of reincarnation. However, until now, such self-awakening has not been permitted except in a few exceptional cases because experiences were much more effective when people were blindfolded. In other words, the earth has been a place to gain experiences through intense emotions, so a clear recognition of the unique circumstances of the earth has not been permitted until beings complete the program.

Beings Who Remember
Everything in the Past

People bitten by dogs in their youth are often afraid of dogs for the rest of their lives, while people who have almost drowned often have difficulty in freeing themselves from a fear of water. While a person raised by loving parents is likely to have a positive attitude toward other people, someone raised by distrustful parents is likely to have difficulty trusting others, especially someone of the opposite sex. Many veterans who fought in the Vietnam War still suffer insomnia or mental disorders, not to mention the physical damage they might be experiencing. In general, people accept that past memories affect present mental states.

Past memories not only influence people mentally, but they also have direct effects on the human body, causing some types of physical suffering such as allergies. For example, a man who suffered from eating a spoiled peach in his childhood may be allergic to peaches for the rest of his life. The memory of the pain caused by the spoiled peach penetrates up to the subconscious level, so that the man's body will automatically reject afterward even the smell of a peach. Similarly, someone who has serious allergies to cats knows right away by their sneezes when a cat is around.

In fact, humans are vastly influenced by their past experiences. However, past memories here refer not only to ones in the present life but also to those from past lives. Every event that ever took place in any past life, and the emotions associated with it, are stored in the human aura.

These stored records surface as strong "feelings" once in a while, inducing diverse emotions like pain and grief. In such cases, however, the surface consciousness does not know what is causing such emotions.

The influence of past-life memories on people can be divided into a few categories. First, past-life memories cause direct pain to the human body. There is a well-known story about the man who often has strong pain in his right shoulder with no known physical cause. Through past-life regression therapy, he discovers that he had died a painful death from a poisonous arrow shot into that shoulder, and the strong memory of pain from that past life appears as a feeling in the present lifetime. According to modern medicine, such pains or diseases that defy medical explanations but still persist may simply be considered to be psychological problems. In truth, however, they are often related to past-life experiences.

Phobias toward certain objects or environments are also caused by the memory of past experiences. Many people have a fear of high places or of enclosed spaces, and often these fears come from past-life memories. Such people may have memories of dying after falling from a high place or of being trapped in confined spaces in previous lives.

Additionally, social phobias or fears of water, fire, or other people result from painful experiences during past lives, too. When I visited Los Angeles in the summer of 2004, I met a woman who had a fear of dying whenever she was in water above her chest. During a past-life regression session, she recalled that she had lived in Thailand about five hundred years ago. During that lifetime, she watched her family members and most people in her village as they were washed away in a flood while she stood in water up to her chest. She of course remembered feeling great sorrow and fear at the time.

In the case of illness related to past-life experiences, rapid improvement or even complete healing can occur just by becoming aware of the cause of the illness. For example, in the case of a patient with unexplained shoulder pain, realizing the fact that the shoulder injury occurred in a past life is the key. At the moment of realization that the cause of pain belongs to a past life, not the present life, the pain may all of a sudden disappear or be reduced greatly. This healing occurs due to the realization that there is no reason to suffer any longer.

Secondly, past-life memories greatly influence personal relationships and material preferences in this lifetime. Individuals experience continuous reincarnation into the material world with others who have had a strong affinity with them in past lives. Despite different appearances and circumstances, relationships with individuals from past lives still have a strong influence in the present life. You could be strongly attracted to or repelled by individuals for no apparent reason, often due to past-life memories.

If you are strongly affected by a certain culture, style, place, or food, it is possibly because you are already accustomed to such things due to your experiences in another lifetime. For example, a person who used to live in Egypt in a past life may be fond of Egyptian hairstyles and clothing in this present life for no apparent reason. Or people in the West who lived in Asia in a past life might be intrigued by Asian people and culture in this life without any apparent cause.

Past-life memories also influence personal tendencies and dispositions in this life. Even if a person was born as a male in this life, he might often exhibit feminine tendencies if he repeatedly chose to live as a female in his past lives. A female who lived as a man many times may often show strong masculine tendencies. A person who used to be active as a warrior or soldier in past lives may demonstrate violent tendencies. A follower of Buddha during the Shakyamuni period probably lived many lives as a Buddhist afterward because of the strong attraction that persists through memory.

In the same manner, a disciple of Christ or of Saint John the Baptist probably repeated many lives as a Christian in his following lives. People with memories of being an animal may frequently show tendencies similar to those of that animal. People who used to exist as plants often prefer plants and nature over human beings.

Thirdly, past-life memories sometimes manifest as special faculties. Past-life memories stored in the human aura can appear during meditation or dreams or can even be directly recalled in some exceptional cases. Although past-life memories usually appear only as vague feelings, it is possible for academic knowledge from past lives to temporarily appear during childhood. As a child grows up, however, such knowledge is likely to be forgotten due to the large quantity of outside information that flows in.

Unlike intellectual knowledge, skills made familiar through the physical body in a past life—such as yoga movement, *gi* practice, artistic abilities, or other sensations of movement—surface easily in the present life. For example, someone who experienced life as a painter over the course of several lifetimes may show artistic talent without much particular effort. A woman who worked as an architectural engineer during the construction of the Egyptian pyramids in a past life may exhibit outstanding talent in geometry during her school years.

More intense experiences in past lives leave stronger memories, thus influencing the present life more intensely. There may be many cases in which someone loved another person in a past life, from whom they were suddenly separated by an accident or death. In these cases, the person carries the painful memory of separation along with a strong longing for the love of the partner. If the person sees the loved one in the next life, strong emotions of love will arise quickly, but there is also an uneasy feeling inside that the love might be suddenly lost again.

The following story is related to one of my own past lives in which I lived as a nobleman about two thousand years ago. In that life, during a horse-riding tour on the eastern coast of the Korean Peninsula, I met an eighteen-year-old girl who was a fisherman's daughter. We loved each other very much for three years until we were separated for some reason. Still in grief and very much in love with me, she refused every wedding proposal and remained alone until her death at the age of forty-eight. In her present life, she retained the same kind of feelings for me. But although she was in love, she had a tremendous fear of separation because of her memories of her previous life. These memories influenced her attitude and behavior towards me immensely and made our relationship very difficult.

People sometimes experience a sudden increase in past-life memories or see flashes of scenes from their past lives during meditations or in dreams. I have witnessed several people who spoke past-life languages fluently during past-life regression, or who repeated the same exact quote uttered in their past lifetime. In particular, I once witnessed a person whose consciousness switched to a past life and remained in that lifetime for a few days without hypnosis. Since all memories are stored in each person's aura, whenever a stimulus is given to a past-life memory or personality, the memories can come to the surface at any time.

It is also fairly common for someone to visit a place he or she used to live in a past life and feel nostalgic or to visualize segments of their life there. Since a part of the person's energy remains in that location, it stimulates or amplifies memories stored inside the aura. During the summer of 2004, I was driving through the plateau area of the Grand Canyon with my daughter, a university student, who was sitting in the passenger seat. During the drive, she saw her past-life figure, who resided in present-day Arizona centuries ago, and she continued to follow his life through vivid scenes on a phantom movie screen.

Everything we experience in past lives is stored, but not with equal significance or strength—so some memories tend to affect people more strongly. When I uploaded an essay entitled "Memories of Lemuria" on my website, I was later told that more than a few people burst into tears after reading it. Some people start to weep whenever they simply hear the word "Lemuria," or their hearts beat rapidly after hearing of the Guides related to the Gaia Project. That can happen because memories of life in Lemuria or as a Guide are strongly engraved into their aura.

In general, past-life memories influence this life to a large degree, as do memories from our past in the present life. In terms of intensity, experiences of this life that are directly stored in our brains as well as in the aura can be more powerful than past-life experiences. However, past-life memories dominate in quantity in comparison to the ones of this life, so their influence is much more powerful than most people realize. In a way, many other past-life personalities coexist with our present one, and in special cases, those personalities can come to the surface. In modern medical science, which does not understand the essence of human beings, this could be diagnosed as mental instability by psychiatrists, and labeled as schizophrenia or as multiple personality disorder.

As discussed above, the notion that the past stays in the past and is irrelevant to the present life is far from the truth. Even right this moment, memories of past lives are directly influencing the present lives of people through their thoughts and emotions. In other words, past-life memories alongside memories of this present life compose the beings we call "Self," so that a human can be defined as a being who responds to the outside world based on all memories of the past. If two beings are different in appearance but contain exactly the same memories, they're the same being. On the other hand, even if two beings look the same, such as identical twins, they still exist as two different beings if their stored memories are different.

Experiencers Living Planned Lives

Each being plans and prepares for the next life while staying in the spiritual world. This plan includes where to be born, how to grow up and whom to grow up to be, whom to meet, what to experience, and how the life will close. However, this life plan for a person is too complex to be completed alone. In order to plan a new life, the individual considers all past lives and decides which new experiences are most urgently needed in the next. Then the available choices are investigated.

For this plan, the individual must know what is going to happen in the third-dimensional world around the time that he or she will live, and what karma needs to be resolved in the next life as well. The individual should also know the relevant rules of reincarnation, and even has to receive in advance the agreement of those people involved in the future life. In addition, there are particular roles that require certain qualifications. Since there are so many elements to take into consideration, life planning cannot be satisfactorily done by an individual. There needs to be help from experts in the fourth-dimensional world.

One of the most important matters in planning a life is the selection of parents to be born to, because an individual's relationship with their parents determines many things that will happen in that person's life. Above all, physical genes are determined, depending on which parents are selected, so this greatly influences physical conditions and predispositions.

It also determines the basic childhood environment, including the home environment and education, which directly influences one's character and to a great extent controls life. As people grow older, they come to think that their decisions are made by free will, but the truth is that decisions are always influenced by preconceived notions and knowledge formed mainly in childhood. In this respect, by selecting parents for the next life, a good portion of one's life plan is completed. It can be said that the outline of a life is put together by the selection of parents and various events of life that humans call "coincidences."

In a society that sets the pursuit of happiness as a first priority, people who experience every day as a burden might ask in disbelief, "Who would plan such a hard life for himself (or herself)?" This is a very natural question for most people, who still look at life from the material point of view while forgetting who they really are. But such a question would disappear for anyone who begins to understand the true meaning of life.

For all beings on the earth, the purpose of life is to experience and learn lessons one by one through experience.

Learning is achieved through experiences of either success or failure, but more and greater learning is achieved as a result of sorrowful and painful experiences than as a result of joyful ones. When a being plans for the next life in the spiritual world, the life plan is created primarily from the viewpoint of learning, without much consideration for physical pain or human happiness. Therefore, experiences of sorrow and pain, if necessary, are chosen and inserted into the playbook of life. There are, of course, many other elements to consider, but the next life is decided from the standpoint of growth of consciousness, and is planned after consideration of the experiences already completed in other lives.

People with opened *hyeols* (or acupuncture points) may occasionally experience déjà vu, but people who have never participated in any special practice or exercise also experience it. Déjà vu is, of course, the phenomenon in which an individual observes a certain scene or experiences something in the present, but has a strong feeling that he or she has already been in that situation before. Déjà vu can happen for various reasons, but sometimes it comes from a memory of an individual's preview of the present life during the life-planning process.

The fact that people themselves plan their lives in advance is not a concept that is easily accepted by most—it is not just difficult for the majority of people to accept, but even those who consider themselves knowledgeable about the invisible world find it hard to believe. Such people may ask how such detailed planning can be done in advance when there are so many different events happening in an individual's life and there are literally countless events occurring in other people's lives at the same time.

Other people may ask how it's possible to plan a life for a certain individual when the whole future of that individual has to be predicted almost perfectly. Some spiritual devotees see scenes of future events by themselves during meditation or in dreams, or find some people with those faculties around them, so they naturally accept the possibility of clairvoyance or prophecy. However, they still wonder how anyone can plan their future in advance.

As people begin to understand how the universe functions, they will soon realize that a future prediction from a high-dimensional world is not that difficult at all. All memories of a being are stored in the being's aura and, furthermore, all events of the universe are perfectly recorded and can be reproduced immediately when necessary. In higher-dimensional worlds of the universe, every being's past memories are fully known and it's understood how those memories will influence the being's thoughts and decisions, so the decisions that the being will make at certain moments can be predicted in advance. Therefore, when important decisions are made in life planning—such as which parents will be chosen, who will be encountered, and what "coincidences" will happen—then the plan for a certain soul's life is nearly complete.

Even though a life is already planned in advance, it does not always follow that a life will proceed exactly as planned. When a soul is in a physical body, the person's memories only exist as vague feelings. Thus, it is somewhat uncertain how those memories will influence the decision-making process. For that reason, so-called human free will plays a big part in human life. Outside energies that humans easily come into contact with, such as thought forms, can also cause one's life to deviate from the primary life plan. (See chapter 7 for more information on this subject.) For these reasons, there is no guarantee that any life will proceed as it was originally planned.

It may sound a little ironic, but when planning a life, the possibility of deviating from the primary plan due to the many variables of life is actually considered. In general, many people live a life and die more or less as planned. Especially for those people who recognize the importance of inner feelings, there is not much possibility of branching away from the original plan. Regardless of what kind of life is planned, each individual's intended life is the best for his or her particular growth of consciousness, so that living a life following inner feelings is important.

The real life of an individual can proceed quite differently from the original plan, but people who were designated for special or important roles are protected and led by spiritual guides to prevent them from missing their primary planned purpose. For the Gaia Project, a large-scale plan for the universe, a great number of high-dimensional beings came to earth in energy form in order to protect the Guides from unexpected occurrences. As the Guides who came to earth as humans are preparing for their missions, the beings in energy bodies protect and guide each of the Guides to continue to live in the way they had planned.

Experiencers of the Unique Earth Energy

Currently, beings of very different frequencies and purposes live together on the earth. In terms of frequencies, all types of beings, from the tenth dimension to the first dimension, are gathered together. The purposes of these beings' visits to earth are extremely varied. Some were sent as the Guides for the Gaia Project, with missions related to the formation, control, and administration of the earth. While some beings came to the earth to enjoy the unique energy and to have various experiences, others came simply because they were attracted to this beautiful blue and green planet. Regardless of the reasons for visiting, anyone who comes to earth feels and learns from the unique earth energy.

From the beginning, the earth was formed specifically to raise the consciousness of the entire galaxy. Thus, it inherently has special energy that other planets do not have and a few distinctive characteristics, including the learning process each being on the earth has been through. Above all, the earth energy accepts and allows everything in the universe. All deeds practiced within the earth's energy are tolerated, understood, and forgiven, which means there is no future disadvantage or punishment for any action or behavior on the material earth. Due to its unique character, the earth has played the role of the perfect place for experiences and for learning. If learning results from those experiences, leading to a rise in consciousness, the experiences cannot be judged as good or bad beforehand.

Learning can be achieved not only from positive thoughts, speech, and behavior, but also from what are usually considered wrong or even sinful thoughts, speech, and behavior. One can learn about the importance of consideration, love, and understanding not only from acts of charity but also from the process of doing the exact opposite: for example, attacking or hurting others due to emotions that boil over. Similarly, one can learn to be considerate, generous, and merciful to others even by experiencing hatred and selfishness. All events on the earth are meaningful from the viewpoint of human experience. Thus, almost all of the achievements or accomplishments about which people usually boast are not very meaningful at all. Learning does occur as a result of accomplishments and successes in life, but even greater learning can come from failure.

The earth has accepted everything so far. However, that does not necessarily mean that every event or deed on the earth has been desirable from the perspective of the earth or the universe. For example, acts of torment, ill-treatment, or hatred towards one's family or neighbors are ill-advised according to any standard. On the earth, which is a place for experience, such deeds have been allowed only because participating in negative activities can eventually make a person learn the importance of consideration and understanding. Also, such behavior is allowed to help an individual to realize the effect of such behavior, and hence to learn to take responsibility for his or her actions.

Another specific characteristic of the earth is its connection with the Origin of the universe. Everything in the universe is laid out by the consciousness of the Origin of the universe so that all beings tend to be alike and get closer to the Origin. However, for beings who lead lives with various roles and experiences, such a connection is not easy to feel on a daily basis. The earth's energy makes all beings long to move toward the Origin.

As I explained in chapter 5, there is another chakra above the seventh chakra, through which people can be connected to the earth's energy. If the consciousness is expanded enough, one can be connected to the earth's energy. While in deep meditation, some spiritual devotees experience a special state of mind in which they feel that they are the universe itself. This "Oneness" experience is possible when one is connected to the earth energy through a temporary leap of consciousness. When one is directly connected to the earth's energy, the mind's capacity increases, and everything in the world is accepted. Through the connection to the earth energy, it is possible to understand that all things in the universe came from one source and are always connected to the Origin.

This special earth energy accepts everything and directs every being closer to the Origin, which is exactly why the earth has been a perfect place for learning from Lemuria up until now.

Beings Who Are Responsible for Their Own Destiny

Many people have a tendency to try and find the causes of their pain and sorrow in others rather than within themselves. People think that their life is the way it is because they had the wrong parents, or they think that business results are bad because of the poor judgment of their boss or subordinates. They may think their life was ruined by a friend, or think they are in a quagmire of confusion because a teacher misguided them. Some extremely depressed or pessimistic people spout bitter feelings and doubt or blame their god or Buddha, or sometimes even perform ceremonies of burning their god at the stake and exclaiming that their god is dead.

On the other hand, people who practice spirituality do not seem to blame others as much for their botched-up lives, but still often feel stifled by not having a clear understanding of life. If there is anyone who deserves to be blamed for the condition of one's life, it is only oneself and nobody else.

As was mentioned earlier, human beings respond to situations based on their accumulated memories of the past. Everything about a being—such as disposition, tendencies, and level of consciousness—comes from the experiences the being has had. However, the memories stored in the aura, which define the individual, have accumulated neither randomly nor accidentally. The experiences from a certain life, and the experiences from the life that follows, proceed from an individual's own plan. In this respect, a human is a being created with one's own free will.

All beings on the earth are supposed to be responsible for themselves. No one on the earth is here against their free will. They all came to the earth by their own choice and have stayed since that time. Their own free will has been reflected in the process of learning, and there is no reason to blame anyone else. When planning one's life, each individual received advice from a counselor in the spiritual world, but basically planned it by himself or herself.

In fact, even after birth, each being had many chances to choose not to live as planned or not achieve the growth in consciousness that the being had in mind, since attitude is decided on by the free will of each individual. Beings who decided that they did not like the material world could choose to stay in the spiritual world without incarnating at all.

In this sense, there is no other person to blame for one's life, and no one else to take responsibility for it. The only person responsible is one's self.

CHAPTER SEVEN
The Meaning of Existence

In this chapter, based on the framework and knowledge established about humans so far, I would like to examine the nature of "beings." Theoretically speaking, it would have been better to examine all beings of the universe before going into detail about humans, but for readers who do not have a clear understanding of human beings, doing so would have made the order of information presented difficult to follow. For that reason, in this book I chose to reverse the order and examine humans first, in chapters 4, 5, and 6, and then, in this chapter, to discuss beings in general, based on the explanations in previous chapters.

So far, we have examined various aspects of humans, human life, and its meaning, but we have not discussed human nature. Everyone who seeks truth should be curious about their own existence and their human entity. Most people define themselves through their physical nature and understand a human in terms of a physical body. On the other hand, most spiritual devotees accept that a human entity is not one that someday disappears, but rather is non-material and never disappears; in Korean, this is called *yeonghon*, meaning "spirit" and "soul." These two English words may be defined differently on occasion, but they will be used interchangeably in this book.

Even if it is accepted that a human entity is a spirit or soul, there are still many ambiguities about what that truly means and how it began. Among various opinions, there is one that claims that numerous souls were brought into existence when the universe was created in a great explosion—an idea running parallel to the Big Bang theory in physics.

There are people who divide the human entity into a substantial one (the "True Self") and a non-substantial one (the "False Self"). Instinctive and negative human properties have been called the False Self, while the high and noble ones have been referred to as the True Self. However, classifying human thoughts and deeds into one of the two categories is an extremely subjective process. The distinction between the False Self and True Self has usually resulted from a human desire not to want to take responsibility for one's undesirable thoughts and actions, or from the human tendency to deflect responsibility onto others. Also, the division between the two Selves depends heavily on religion, culture, and social values. Therefore, the demarcation between the two Selves is just a concept of convenience.

The easiest way to understand the nature of all beings is to see them from a cognitive point of view. All beings of the universe, including humans, are cognitive. The most basic form of cognition is to identify oneself as being separate from others, and cognition progresses gradually to complex cognition. Beings that possess such cognitive faculties can be called consciousness or conscious bodies.

In this chapter, I explain the birth and evolution of consciousness. I also examine the relationship among humans, animals, and plants, and the relationship between the Higher Self and the Subordinate Self. Finally, I examine thought forms that have greatly influenced the human world.

Birth and the Evolution of Consciousness

Most spiritual devotees agree that the mind is the subject of life. A large proportion of human life is devoted to thinking and making decisions from moment to moment. However, as mentioned earlier, the mind can be largely divided into two aspects. One aspect includes rather passive properties such as moods, emotions, instincts, or feelings, which cannot be controlled by one's self. These properties derive from having a physical body, from the memories of past experiences, or through connection with outside energy.

The other aspect includes rather active properties, which either demonstrate or embody each individual's inherent, independent will, and have usually been called consciousness. Consciousness can be defined as the faculty of a being who perceives the world and creates something out of that perception. From this viewpoint, the nature of being, including that of human beings, can be described as consciousness.

The birth of consciousness and the process of its proliferation is exactly how the universe came to form and develop, which can be explained through the concepts of *mu-geuk* and *tae-geuk* (both Korean terms), presented by Taeho Bokhi (Fu His) about fifty-six hundred years ago. Before the very beginning of the present universe, there was a state of absolute stillness. This state, known as *mu-geuk*, existed without any consciousness, but had within it the potential of all conceptions. A very subtle movement began one moment, breaking the long silence. And the imminent energy inside *mu-geuk* assembled slowly, forming a circle that began to turn. And with this, the very first *tae-geuk*, or the first systematic power, appeared.

As the *tae-geuk* formed and began to turn, the imminent power began to collect in a mass around the *tae-geuk*. The rotation speed grew faster and the circle grew bigger. As the rotation continued, the first *tae-geuk* grew into a huge circle rotating with tremendous speed. With its enormous rotating power, parts of it broke off at one moment and formed other *tae-geuks* that began rotating themselves. Just as the original *tae-geuk* (*bon-tae-geuk* in Korean) did, the power and the speed of rotation of the newly-born *tae-geuks* gradually increased, and as they reached a certain level, they began to create other circles like themselves. Through such a process, a great number of large and small *tae-geuks* were created and began to rotate throughout the universe.

Here, *bon-tae-geuk* represents the power of the Origin of the universe, and each *tae-geuk* represents an individual consciousness or the power that creates consciousness. After spinning off the very first five rotating *tae-geuks*, the *bon-tae-geuk* stopped its own rotation and movement. The five *tae-geuks* that were formed directly from the *bon-tae-geuk* were the first consciousnesses in the universe. That is, they are the consciousness of the Origin in the tenth dimension. All the other *tae-geuks* in the entire universe now were generated directly by one or more of the first consciousnesses. As the universe is continuously expanding, the number of consciousnesses has been increasing. This is a brief summary of how the consciousness of the universe appeared and how it was separated into so many consciousnesses afterward.

However, the actual creation process of each consciousness by the first consciousness is not uniform. Depending on its purpose, its dimension, and the intended characteristics of the consciousness, there are differences in many aspects—such as which beings of the Origin are involved, how important a role each creator plays, and what kind of process is taken.

In the creation of the very first ninth-dimensional being, all five beings of the Origin took part in the process. The same was true in the creation of the holy being for the Gaia Project, although the third being of the Origin had a leading role of the process. On the other hand, most consciousnesses are created by only one being of the Origin.

For a recent creation of a special seventh-dimensional being, the third being of the Origin took center position, but other beings—including many ninth-dimensional energy experts—also participated in the grand ceremony and contributed their energies to the birth process. In comparison, fourth-dimensional beings and lower are created in groups, depending on what is needed in the universe. In one case, fourth-dimensional beings were born simultaneously in a circle, some beings larger than the others. When third-dimensional beings are created, however, they are usually much more uniform in size.

Through such a process, consciousnesses of numerous and various frequencies were generated, and in the same dimension those formed earlier in the process tended to have higher frequencies of vibration. Although each consciousness has a different speed of expansion because of different preferences for new experiences, the ones created earlier had more experiences, and hence further expanded their consciousness and raised their frequency. All beings in the universe have constantly been expanding their consciousnesses through continuous experiences. Since the consciousness of the Origin includes all consciousnesses, the constant expansion of each individual consciousness leads to the expansion of the consciousness of the Origin, and the expansion of the universe itself.

Some might be curious about what existed before *mu-geuk* or how the very first movement came about, but this is not a meaningful question. The very first consciousness of the universe was formed when *bon-tae-geuk* started its rotation. For this reason, any meaningful discussion about what existed before the formation of the very first consciousness is not possible.

Animals and Plants

Many people no doubt regard the comparison of human beings with animals and plants to be an insult to the human race or a challenge to human dignity. This reaction comes from the belief that the nature of humans is completely different from that of animals and plants. Even many of those who pursue spirituality consider humans to be far superior to animals or to plants in substantial, spiritual respects. However, this belief stems from a serious misunderstanding of existence and is far from the truth.

Recently, it has been scientifically proven that not only animals such as whales but also plants have cognitive faculties similar to those of humans. Research into the cognitive faculties of plants is still in the preliminary stages, but there is somewhat convincing evidence suggesting that plants, including trees, communicate among themselves using waves or other methods.

Some plants generate poisonous substances to defend themselves when faced with danger, and send warning signals to friends by spreading chemical substances. Plants also have constant interaction with people. Most gardeners are aware that the more love and attention they give to plants, the fresher, stronger, and faster their plants will grow. Some wildflowers, thickets, and trees not only help to raise people's consciousnesses through high-frequency energy, but they also offer pathways through which spiritual messages from the universe can be received.

In this respect, classification of beings on the earth by physical appearance is quite different from classification based on the beings' spiritual essence. A more meaningful classification system would be one organized by the frequencies of individual beings. Beings with first- or second-dimensional frequencies have a smaller capacity to store information. They are relatively simple in terms of their cognitive faculties and thinking processes, so their cognition of the world is limited. From this perspective, it is natural that beings of higher frequencies tend to be born as humans in order to have more complicated experiences. On the other hand, beings of lower frequencies may in general be reincarnated as small animals or plants first in order to have simpler experiences, and then appear as humans after sufficient experiences. It is not possible for a being of a first-dimensional frequency to be born and live as a human.

Since earth has been operated as a perfect place for experiences, it has so far accepted any being from the universe, and the free will of each individual has been respected to a maximum level. When the earth was materialized for the first time, the choice to be born as a human, an animal, or a plant was given to all beings as long as they met the minimum requirements for levels of frequency. Such a choice was offered so that each being could have unique experiences by living as their chosen life form in the material world, and so that each being could be reincarnated in a different life form in their next life if they so desired.

However, as time passed, the rules of reincarnation concerning humans, animals, and plants changed. As all beings on the materialized earth experienced a lapse of memory, their appearances and abilities became very important. Animals were often mistreated or slaughtered, and plants were ignored as insignificant beings. Although the karma system demanded responsible behavior from every being from the beginning of the materialization, the phenomenon of humans treating animals and plants contemptuously worsened. For that particular reason, many beings who came to the earth wanted to be reincarnated as humans. In particular, violent beings with domination tendencies preferred to be reincarnated as human beings.

In accordance with such changes in preferences, the system of reincarnation also made adjustments. In the beginning of the materialization, based on preferences, each being could be reincarnated as a human, an animal, or a plant if their frequency allowed it. Later, however, a being's life form in the next life also began to be determined by its previous deeds. In other words, karma as well as the individual's frequency was figured into the complex rules of reincarnation when choosing life forms.

There are beings who are reincarnated as animals or plants that have inherently higher frequencies than most human beings, and many beings who are born as humans now have lower frequencies than certain animals or plants. Past-life regressions I have done show that beings of very high-dimensional frequencies, who are reincarnated as humans now, had indeed lived as animals or plants in their past lives.

Viewed not from the surface or material level but from a more fundamental level, the basic difference among life forms is their ability to learn. When born as a human, even if one has a low frequency of vibration, a person is mobile and has the ability to gain various experiences in the vast human world. However, animals and plants are stationed in a limited area and their experiences take place under circumstances they can't control, in which their will or intentions are irrelevant. In particular, plants, which cannot move around, mainly learn from interaction with nature, and, through endless waiting, learn patience and tolerance.

It is therefore necessary to be reincarnated as a human if a being wants greater expansion of consciousness. While most animals, including primates, are individual beings, insects and plants exist as a sort of collective consciousness. That is, a being born as an animal experiences individual existence, while insects and plants do not.

In the case of humans, people with frequencies of the third dimension or lower mainly perceive the material world from a narrow perspective, incapable of perceiving the nonmaterial world and that which exists beyond. A relatively small number of people with higher frequencies perceive both worlds, and thus are dissatisfied with material reality. Such people often encounter serious difficulties in life and have a hard time adjusting to their surroundings.

Beings with higher frequencies are easily found among certain animals and plants, such as very old trees, whales, or turtles. People will begin to see the world from a completely different perspective from the moment they realize that all living beings on the earth are consciousnesses, and that humans are not necessarily superior to other life forms at their essence.

The Higher Self and the Subordinate Self

Quite unlike the creation by the first consciousness of the universe, there are cases in which an individual consciousness duplicates itself to produce another self. To be precise, original beings of higher dimensions sometimes duplicate themselves in order to send the duplicates to lower-dimensional worlds for special purposes. In these cases, the original being is called the Higher Self, and the duplicated being, which is sent to the earth or another lower-dimensional place, is called the Subordinate Self or Lower Self.

For example, among beings who came to the earth as Guides of the Gaia Project, there are many cases in which their Higher Selves are on stars of the fifth dimension or higher. High-dimensional consciousnesses in the universe can create between three and six duplicates to conduct several activities in different places at the same time. There are even cases in which two or more Subordinate Selves were sent to the earth to live different lives.

The Higher Self and the Subordinate Self are basically one entity, and they share the same memories. Despite the fact that the Subordinate Self does not have all the memories of the Higher Self, it does hold all of their basic memories in common. After the duplication process, the Subordinate starts to accumulate experiences that the Higher Self does not have. So, in order to keep the one entity, new information accumulated by the Subordinate Self is regularly copied and transferred to the Higher Self.

For Subordinate Selves who are reincarnated on the material earth, however, the relationship is a bit different. Due to the environment of the materialized earth, the being located on the earth can exhibit thinking and behavior that is quite different from that of the Higher Self. The difference is a result of at least several reasons, including no direct connection or communication between the two, a lapse of memory of the previous existence, physical desires from the material body, and so on. For such reasons, most of the Subordinate Selves on the earth have been living until now with no knowledge of their Higher Selves elsewhere in the universe.

All the basic information is held in common between the Higher Self and the Subordinate Self, and between one Subordinate and another Subordinate. Thus, even though they have different appearances and reside in different environments, surprising similarities can exist between them in terms of taste, manner, and way of thinking, and they may even show hints of similarity in appearance. There was a case during a past-life regression in which the physical characteristics of a person on the earth were very similar to his Higher Self on Sirius. I have also encountered a case of great similarity between two people on the earth who share the same

Higher Self. One was born and lives in Korea while the other lives in New Zealand, but they show striking similarities in terms of skin color, appearances, tastes, and mannerisms.

A Higher Self, who has sent another self to the earth either to carry out its mission related to the Gaia Project or to gain experiences, usually does not get involved in the life of the Subordinate Self, but merely observes it. However, there are cases where the Higher Self is actively involved in the life of the Subordinate Self in order to make the Subordinate one aware of the original being and to prepare for the mission. The Higher Selves send messages to the Subordinate Selves mostly through dreams or moments of unconsciousness during meditation. They sometimes generate special spiritual experiences or make a direct appearance in some way.

Thought Forms Created by Human Beings

Besides the consciousnesses that are all directly created by the consciousness of the Origin, there are other beings that are actively cognizant of themselves and the world. These are "thought forms" created by the human mind. Understanding what thought forms are and how they are created or disappear will increase understanding of the purification process during the earth's Great Change discussed in chapter 2 as well as the history of humans on the earth explained in chapter 4.

As discussed in chapter 5, humans have the ability to control *gi* (or the energy of the universe) by using the mind. Visualizations in the mind immediately result in creations in the fourth-dimensional energy world. Imagination or prayer with continuous concentration creates an energy body that becomes alive. Thought forms are created through this process. Especially when a large group of people pray for the same wish collectively, the created thought form acts as a powerful energy body and greatly influences people who have thoughts similar to those who created it.

Thought forms can directly influence or even dominate people's thinking, and they can cause completely unexpected thoughts or behavior in humans. People have been aware of their weaknesses for a long time, and have relied on the existence of the powerful when they ardently desired abundance in life. Such desires and behaviors created various energy bodies even without people noticing them. In particular, religious or spiritual groups whose members believe in the same absolute being have created strong thought forms as a result of their collective prayers or chanting.

Thought forms created in this way often affect people with certain belief systems and participants of certain meetings or rituals. By blocking individuals' independent rational judgment, thought forms drive people's thoughts in a particular direction. In some cases, they even induce a sort of hypnotic state. There are many cases in which thought forms have cleverly controlled people's consciousness by presenting special spiritual experiences or by appearing in dreams as special beings. When people claim to have seen Jesus Christ, the Buddha, the Goddess of Mercy, or the Virgin Mary in dreams or during meditation, there is a strong possibility that it was really a trick of thought forms.

Thought forms created by certain groups can help achieve the goals or actions of the group by dominating or controlling the minds of its members. If a member of a group is dedicated to the group, the thought forms may help the person both materially and morally, or present a somewhat special ability, such as the power to read other people's minds.

On the other hand, if a person doubts or decides to leave the group, the thought forms may disturb the person by giving various kinds of mental and physical pain that will hold that person back from leaving the group. Since thought forms are supplied with energy from people's minds, they become weaker or even extinct if fewer people sympathize with them. Once thought forms are created, they keep interfering with human consciousness by stirring up fears and uneasy feelings—because thought forms worry that the growth of people's consciousnesses will weaken humans' dependency on the thought forms and therefore weaken the thought forms' domination of the human world.

Though there are some thought forms that are very forceful due to their being the shared desires of many people, such thought forms are quite different from humans, animals, and plants in terms of the purpose of their formation and their growth process. In general, consciousness is a being who was created by one of the original beings of the universe and has grown with its unique experiences after the creation, and the being's existence never depends on the outside world. On the other hand, thought forms are energy bodies that are created by human minds and become active only for specific goals. Thus, there is no growth of consciousness for them or for anything similar, and they will disappear when they are cut off from the human mind. However, their strength can greatly increase when people's desires become stronger or when more people participate in the activities that create and nourish the thought forms.

CHAPTER EIGHT
Growth of Consciousness

Almost every system of modern society has been based on self-centeredness and competitiveness, and has constantly encouraged competition among society members. Communism and socialism, both of which sought to establish an ideal society for humans, were tested on the earth for a while, but they deteriorated. With the establishment of capitalism, based on the egoistic human mind, the world was transformed into an extremely competitive society rushing for more materialistic growth at a frightful speed. The goal of life for an absolute majority of people has become to possess or enjoy as many material things as possible. Such thoughts and deeds of people match well with the market economy, which results in great material achievement and maximum competitiveness in human societies.

It seems that many spiritual devotees accept such a competitive principle even for spiritual growth. They think that human society is a competitive society anyway, so spiritual growth among people can be accelerated through competition. Based on their understanding of spirituality and their discovery of the value in seeking after truth, such devotees make an effort to reach a higher level or achieve greater enlightenment by practicing harder than others. On the other hand, there are others, especially people with New Age tendencies, who turn away from human society's constant competition for superiority and deny any authority. Instead, they emphasize that every human is a part of God and that we are all one.

Human history so far has shown that the general public has always been trampled on and used by those with power and authority. It is thus natural that some ascetic devotees have a tendency to deny all kinds of authority. However, if support of the material and secular authority is one extreme, disregarding all authority may be the other extreme. In every kind of society on the earth, including human society, there is a certain power source from which public order is maintained. Until now, political, economic, and religious authorities have served that purpose. On the other hand, the universe, except the earth, has been managed harmoniously in a fundamentally different way—in other words, by connectivity with the Origin.

As was discussed in chapters 1 and 7, every being in the universe was created by at least one of the beings of the Origin for a specific purpose, and each being could, until now, be differentiated from other beings in terms of original frequency of vibration and accumulated experiences. It appears that the original frequency or dimension that determines a being's capacity for perception is the most important characteristic of that being. However, all the original properties, including the frequency of each being, were given by the Origin to fulfill a certain purpose and to make the being perform a specific role. It is therefore impossible to say which role is more important or which being is more valuable.

It is true that the original frequency generates many differences in appearance, including each being's role, and that there seems to be a clear spiritual hierarchy or spiritual order based on frequencies. However, in the universe outside the earth, where all beings see each other not by their appearance but in their substance, there is naturally no discrimination at all among beings as there is on the earth. All the beings come from one source—in other words, the same Origin, and hence they are all siblings. Instead of discrimination similar to that found among people on the earth, there is brotherhood and sisterhood, love, and harmony in the universe.

In that respect, the concept of spiritual evolution and expansion of consciousness, in which many ascetic devotees have believed until now, needs to be modified somewhat. Spiritual evolution or expansion of consciousness implies there is a need to keep learning, to increase one's true knowledge about the infinite universe. It is not something one being can achieve in a competitive environment, but something that can be naturally achieved along the path of life. As discussed above, since each being was created to perform a specific role, it is very rare in the universe that a continual expansion of consciousness brings a being to a higher dimension. In this respect, the earth's

Great Change, which will offer some beings the opportunity to rise to a higher dimension, is a very exceptional phenomenon in the universe.

Recently among many ascetic devotees, interest in the level of human consciousness and expansion of consciousness has increased. In this chapter, I will discuss the expansion of consciousness, and I will examine the concept of consciousness levels that was introduced by David Hawkins, the author of *Power vs. Force*.

Differences by Level of Consciousness

Since the formation of the universe, all beings of the universe have gone their own way, each piling up unique memories. During the lifetime of a physical human being, some of the memories stored in the aura can be transmitted in the form of feelings, and these constantly influence the decisions that are made. For this reason, two friends from childhood or two brothers can have very different perspectives on life and the universe. Perspectives on the world are built up based on all past experiences and accumulated information up until the present moment, so even two people living together during the same time period and acquiring the same knowledge can see the world very differently. In short, each individual has a unique way of viewing the world.

If a person has accumulated many experiences from the earth as well as from other stars in the universe, it means that the being has moved closer to the Origin of the universe. Thus, it would be natural for the person to attach more importance to harmony and fellowship than do others with lower consciousness levels. In this respect, even though they live on the materialized earth, beings with higher levels of consciousness exhibit a strong tendency to value the importance of harmony, peace, and consideration for neighbors.

David Hawkins tried to standardize these different viewpoints of the world using the concept of consciousness levels. According to Hawkins, as the level of consciousness goes up, people move away from helplessness or fear, and instead come to embrace others with courage. As the level rises further, people experience love and joy, and sometimes feel absolute peace.

However, it is not the case that people have the same particular dispositions in accordance with their consciousness level, nor is it the case that people's speech and behavior are always directly related to their consciousness level. It is true, however, that humans' disposition, speech, and behavior usually have quite a close relationship with their consciousness level, but there is not a direct cause and effect relationship between consciousness level and disposition, speech, and behavior.

Even if a being has a relatively high consciousness level because of many accumulated experiences, his or her speech and behavior may naturally exhibit negative tendencies if the being's experiences are mainly negative and violent. On the other hand, even though a being has a relatively low consciousness level due to a small volume of experiences accumulated, if the experiences are mainly positive and cheerful, the being's behavior is likely to be very positive. In this respect, judging people's consciousness levels based on their dispositions can lead to big mistakes. Consciousness is something that can be expanded as a result of either positive experiences or negative experiences.

People often think that the disposition of a certain person is mainly formed by education or home environment during this lifetime, but that is not the case. Instead, the fundamental disposition of a person is influenced mostly by past-life experiences, especially by the experiences on the star where the being stayed for a long time. For example, beings who stayed in the Pleiades before coming to the earth usually exhibit feminine and sensitive dispositions, while beings from Sirius tend to be more systematic, organized, and rational. That is the case because the Pleiades is a star cluster with warm, feminine energy that emphasizes care for and special consideration toward others, while Sirius is the star on which the administrative center of the galaxy is located. In addition, some people who exhibit strong violent tendencies are likely to have come from stars that experienced endless vicious wars.

Most people find it difficult to determine someone's consciousness level, since the level may not be revealed and cannot be judged by one's speech or behavior. If there is a great difference in the consciousness levels among people, some obvious differences might appear in many aspects, including fundamental ways of thinking about the material world versus the non-material, self-centeredness, jealousy, envy, love, and caring. However, a relatively small difference in consciousness level would not manifest in outward characteristics. Instead, differences in the consciousness level create significant differences in attitudes toward the unknown—that is, the aspect of recognizing the possibility of something new.

A being who has accumulated many experiences both on the earth and in outer space does not judge impulsively, but is open to various possibilities even for a seemingly obvious case. This is because the being knows from long experience that the world is full of surprises. On the other hand, a being who has accumulated relatively few past-life memories judges rather quickly and exhibits a more decisive disposition. This behavior can be seen as an unconscious way of protecting oneself. When people encounter more information than is in their capacity to digest, and try hard to force themselves to accept it, an extreme state of confusion might result, which could develop into a mental disorder. For that reason, people close the gates of their minds to information that greatly exceeds their consciousness levels. That also explains why a person with a lower consciousness level usually discriminates more and shows more decisive behavior.

As mentioned before in relation to dimensions, a higher frequency or a higher level of consciousness means a larger capacity for holding information. However, the frequency or consciousness level should not be considered in connection with the value of a being. Countless beings play their own roles in the universe, and the universe runs smoothly because of these various beings who play their own roles. Although it is true that beings of lower frequencies are usually playing simpler roles, it does not necessarily mean that they are less valuable.

Expansion of Consciousness

The most important topic among spiritual devotees has always been the growth of consciousness and the quest for enlightenment. Many people think that such achievement can only be accomplished through special deeds associated with spiritual practices. That is, they think that spiritual evolution, or ultimate enlightenment, can be achieved only after very long hours of practice, including Zen Buddhist meditation or other types of meditation, asceticism, or charitable acts. These people think that a rise in consciousness cannot take place as a result of mundane everyday life or through experiencing various emotions such as joy, anger, sorrow, and pleasure. They sometimes even worry that experiences that cause such emotions may lower their consciousness levels.

However, expansion of consciousness means that the volume of information accumulated by learning has gone up and that the frequency corresponding to the volume has moved up to a higher level. So an expansion of consciousness can be accomplished not only by deeds associated with ascetic practices, but also as a result of every type and every moment of experience. In other words, it can be said that life itself is ascetic practice and everything remembered through experiences assists in expanding consciousness.

The most important consideration for the expansion of consciousness is not about how or what kind of life a person lives, but rather about how a person spends each moment of life. More focus on each moment of life brings stronger experiences, which are left as more powerful memories, expanding the person's consciousness faster. For instance, when some sadness or pain approaches you, if you bravely experience it instead of trying to avoid it, then your level of consciousness grows much more.

On the other hand, if you are constantly obsessing about the past or are preoccupied with worry about the future instead of focusing on the present, even a long experience on the earth is not so helpful, and a great expansion of consciousness cannot take place.

In this respect, many methods of ascetic or spiritual practice that have been developed and handed down to us until now need to be reconsidered. It seems that many of the methods were developed based on a superficial understanding of life and with no profound understanding of humans and human consciousness. They seem to focus on how to bring peace to a constantly trembling mind in the belief that ascetic practice pacifies the mind and is the only way to realize a rise in consciousness and ultimately reach enlightenment. Some groups even teach people to repeatedly erase all accumulated memories.

However, as discussed before, a person is accumulated memory itself. Erasing a person's memories means obliterating his or her own existence; such effort is not advisable, and in fact it is not even possible. It would be good to purify and resolve the emotions generated from the memories, but erasing the valuable learning that took place through experience is to deny the meaning of human beings.

People who focus on such practices may temporarily experience a state in which all thinking stops, and all feelings about the world and all kinds of agonizing emotions disappear. But as time passes, all sorts of memories, including emotions, are revived. This kind of forceful method of practice represses an expanding consciousness while at the same time interferes with new and various experiences of life. People can temporarily find peace of mind through various methods of practice for the mind, but such methods may never lead to expansion of consciousness or make people move any closer to genuine enlightenment.

For a person with a high-dimensional consciousness who has been living an ordinary life, a sudden expansion of consciousness can happen either from everyday life or while participating in spiritual practices. Such a person may begin to feel a continuous fine vibration in the body and have a faint sense that the body is surrounded by an energy membrane. To that person, everything seems like a dream and it sometimes becomes impossible to think with the brain. Such a phenomenon takes place when a high-level energy or the earth energy is connected to the person. As a result of such experiences, such an individual can rapidly recover the original consciousness level.

While witnessing such phenomena, some spiritual devotees believe that these types of special practices or experiences can make a person's consciousness jump a level, but this is not at all true. The sudden expansion of consciousness for some truth seekers is what they recovered of the original level of consciousness. It is not a genuine growth of consciousness. A true expansion of consciousness takes place very slowly, little by little, with the accumulation of learning through experiences. It can never be achieved in a short time.

Also, some spiritual devotees worry that if they do not practice hard enough in this life, they may move backward spiritually instead of forward. But this thought is also mistaken. Even if a person ends this life at a low level of consciousness without recovering the original level, the person's stored memories will never disappear. So the original frequency—that is, the original consciousness of the being—will never decline.

PART THREE

BEING PREPARED FOR THE COSMIC FESTIVITIES

INTRODUCTION TO PART THREE

People on the material earth have indeed been "frogs in a well." Most people, including myself until not long ago, have lived with the belief that this material world is the only one that exists. Even if there is an invisible world, people think, it must be beyond our comprehension, so that any effort to grasp the real meaning of life and the universe will not bring any meaningful results. In some sense, accepting the possibility that there are numerous other worlds unfolding infinitely beyond the material one makes people uncomfortable, so most refuse to think about it.

The deep ignorance of the real world among humans is peculiar to the material earth, in which all the memories of past lives as well as of the fourth-dimensional spiritual world are buried in deep storage at the time of physical reincarnation. Before reincarnating into the physical world, beings knew, at least somewhat, about themselves and the system of reincarnation. But at the moment humans begin their lives on the earth with physical bodies, they fall into a deep oblivion. Due to a material curtain hung in front of human beings, the deeply-stored truth could not be revealed until now. Although it is true that many people had to undergo great pain and endure stifling feelings as a result of such oblivion, it is also true that beings could learn more effectively that way.

However, the situation has changed. It is time for all humankind to know about the real world and for all the truth to be revealed completely through the light entering from above. We are at the final stage of the Gaia Project and all the residents on this planet are now about to graduate from the very special school, the so-called earth.

In order to make the graduation ceremony very memorable and very rewarding for all graduating students, preparations need to be made by the students as well as by the school administration. As for the students, it is necessary that they get beyond their "frogs in a well" mentality. Instead of seeking comfort from existing knowledge and their preconceived notions, they must open their minds widely and be ready to accept the possibility of the new revelations of life, the earth, and the universe discussed in this book.

In this part, by discussing how reliable your existing knowledge really is, how much influence preconceived notions have on you, and how this book was written, I present several reasons why you can trust this book and why you should open your mind to these new possibilities. I also discuss what can be done at this moment in preparation for the Great Change, and what can be achieved during this special period.

CHAPTER NINE
Preparations for the Great Change

Due to the "frogs in a well" mentality, the perspectives and attitudes of people toward life do not easily change, especially under usual circumstances. These perspectives and attitudes may change only when people experience something very profound such as the death of a loved one or a fatal disease. Even for spiritual devotees who spend most of their time in meditation or in some other types of ascetic practice, fundamental change often only comes as the result of unique or shocking events and experiences.

The earth's Great Change will provide a precious opportunity for special experiences, which can lead people to fundamental changes in their attitudes toward life and even toward so-called enlightenment. Many people will be awakened by witnessing various phenomena occurring as part of the purification of the earth. As they watch the material world that they have valued so much collapse around them and see every authority vanish without exerting any power to stop what is happening, people will have a chance to look back on their materialistic lives.

At first glance, the earth's Great Change will seem to be a horrible catastrophe to many people, but later it will be recognized as the last precious opportunity for special learning for all beings who have stayed on the earth until now. They will realize by themselves that what is taking place on the earth is not accidental at all, but rather it is a part of the careful plan of the universe—a cosmic blessing for the people of the earth. Such a realization will provide a chance to remember their own origins and greatly expand their consciousnesses.

Among those who are reading this book, no doubt many are still enamored with materialism and are not ready to seek the truth of human nature and its origins. However, others will start to recognize the fact that the contents in this book are too specific and too systematic to be easily denied. In particular, a considerable number of readers may take the changes occurring on the earth seriously and so accept a good portion of this book.

Such readers will begin to understand that the common goal of all beings on the earth is to extend their learning and expand their consciousnesses through various experiences. Readers may be awakened enough to understand the uniqueness of the earth and to realize that people on this planet are now at a special moment in the earth's entire history. They—perhaps you—may agree that earth's Great Change, now in progress, will provide tremendous experiences unparalleled throughout the entire universe, and that it will be the best opportunity yet for any individual to greatly expand his or her consciousness.

However, among those readers who accept a certain possibility that the Gaia Project is real, many may wonder what specifically they should do now. Although they may have already noticed that everything must have been prepared by the Project administration and there may be nothing each individual has to prepare for, they still might feel as if there must be helpful practices or desirable ways of life at this special point in time.

In this chapter, I will discuss what can be done by each individual to prepare for the earth's Great Change. I insist that the most important and the most urgent preparation for the Great Change is to read this book thoroughly and to understand the contents as fully as possible. When people witness social chaos and natural disasters with a good understanding of the Gaia Project, their initial fright will be changed to a realization of the real meaning of life, and ultimately to joy and gratitude. Without an understanding of the Gaia Project, however, the blessed experiences cannot happen at all.

To make people open their minds and accept a new possibility more easily, it seems necessary to discuss the reliability of existing knowledge and the problems of preconceived notions. Also, to help readers better evaluate this book and judge its trustworthiness, it may be helpful to know in detail how this book was written. Through these discussions, the Gaia Project will appear to you as a real possibility. I also discuss what else can be done, and whether or not spiritual practices are helpful at this point in time.

How Reliable Is Our Existing Knowledge?

Taking a cosmic point of view, this book explains the earth, humans, and the earth's Great Change that is now in progress, and provides insight into life on the earth and its history. The contents of this book may be confusing, or they might be rejected by many people, because a good portion of the book is very different not only from general intuition, agreed-upon "common sense," or scientific knowledge, but also from other spiritual teachings or existing religious doctrines. In particular, the history of earth and humankind revealed in this book is very different from established historical knowledge, so that even relatively open-minded readers might be quite confused at first.

Thus, to understand and evaluate this book properly, it seems necessary to reconsider what we as humans have always accepted as the truth, and to reexamine what we've mindlessly been taught to believe and have taken in as fact. As a relevant example from this book, consider again the history of the earth and humans discussed in chapter 4. Although you may resist accepting the history revealed in that chapter as fact, your attitude toward that history will dramatically change when you become familiar with how known and agreed-upon history is really written.

In fact, the history we know is questionable not only from the standpoint of what really happened but also from the perspective of when historical events actually took place. There seems to be especially serious difficulties in estimating the correct dates of remains or ruins. Every time new remains or ruins are excavated, geologists, archeologists, and historians estimate their dates using various techniques and often revise the existing history of the earth and humanity. However, the techniques used to estimate dates seem to be very primitive and hard to trust. Often, the difference in estimated dates arrived at by different techniques is too great for anyone to accept any one of the estimates, and differences in results among the techniques increase greatly for something very old, implying that estimation of true history by analyzing remains or ruins is, in fact, impossible.

In addition to the problem of accurately dating ruins or remains, there is a serious problem concerning the reliability of historical records. Even in our modern era with its highly developed communications and mass media, the truth is still not always revealed to the public, suggesting that the reliability of older historical records is indeed questionable.

Perhaps the history we know may not be correct from the very beginning. The reality until now has been that once a doctrine has been established as a theory, any new discovery afterwards must be made to fit into that theory. If not, new findings and new scholarship are easily rejected in academic circles.

Taking such a situation into consideration, we find a strong possibility that the system of history that the general public accepts is distorted. Many aspects of written history may not be correct, or even history as we know it might be fundamentally wrong. Archeology based on a few remains and ruins without any solid historical record is not really a science but an art—a literary work linked together with very fragmentary evidence and the imagination of historians.

Once you acknowledge this fact about existing history and archeological knowledge, you may experience a completely new horizon of consciousness when reading this book.

We should also consider the reliability problem of "common sense" or scientific knowledge in general. In almost all academic areas, empirical studies based on statistics are emphasized. In the medical field and in psychology, for example, the conditions of all patients are dichotomized into "normal" and "abnormal" by using diverse statistical techniques. Being normal originally meant that a certain feature or condition was found in the majority of people, and being abnormal meant that a feature or condition was found only in a minority of people. But, in the absence of a reliable theory or thorough understanding of the human body and human mind, these terms have come to mean that a certain feature or condition is "good" or "bad."

A patient's diagnosis is usually based on this dichotomized analysis of symptoms, and efforts are often made to change an "abnormal" condition to a "normal" condition without knowing the basic cause or reason for a symptom. Because modern medical science has been developed based on treatment of symptoms rather than as a result of real knowledge of humans and the human body, it is very rare to detect an exact cause or reason for a medical symptom. Thus, a typical doctor's diagnosis is not based on an exact cause or disease, but rather on the symptoms of a patient. In most cases, doctors apply various medical methods one at a time in order to treat the symptoms, usually trying the one that has been proven to be the most effective in laboratory experiments first, until the symptoms disappear. A similar situation exists in other academic areas. In sum, modern science is, in general, not based on real facts but rather on hypotheses or academic assumptions that are continuously being replaced by new ones.

Despite the current state of science, most people are very receptive to so-called scientific findings, and any hypothesis or theory announced by a known scholar is easily accepted as fact or truth, and soon becomes accepted as established knowledge or common sense. Of course, the public trust in modern science is not groundless. As a matter of fact, the great public trust in scientists is based largely on their brilliant achievements during the twentieth century; their work has provided the theoretical backbone of the progress of material civilization. However, in reality, most branches of science have not reached a level at which they are able to explain the fundamental causes of phenomena occurring on the earth or in the human body. Not realizing this fact, people often put too much trust in, and overemphasize, science and existing knowledge.

One side effect of putting too much trust in science is that people tend not to open their minds to truth when it is revealed. This situation is especially true regarding the invisible worlds that scientists currently have no means to detect or analyze. However, the fact that the invisible world is beyond the grasp of modern science does not mean that people should distrust non-scientific approaches or their results. It implies rather that when readers try to judge the truthfulness of or evaluate a book beyond the reach of science, it is not appropriate to examine whether or not its content is compatible with any existing scientific knowledge.

Ascetic spiritual devotees may not easily accept this book for a different reason: because most of its contents are not compatible with existing spiritual teachings, and some are even contradictory to them. Because this book explains the unlimited and overlapping universe as clearly as if one were looking into a crystal ball, it may be baffling for many spiritual devotees who have accepted the assertion that truth cannot be expressed properly in any human language. It has been said that once truth is spoken, it is no longer the truth.

However, as anyone who has had the experience of studying a subject in depth already knows, the more deeply and the more clearly one understands a certain matter, the more accurately and specifically one can describe it. Thus, even though it is true that no current human language is rich enough to fully describe the truth of the universe, such linguistic limitations do not justify very ambiguous statements about cosmic truth.

From the readers' viewpoint, among many different claims about specific aspects of human history or invisible worlds, there is no easy way to figure out which ones are right and which ones are wrong. However, one thing is clear: if explanations are somewhat contradictory within themselves and are not self-sustaining, on the whole they cannot be true. Thus, to some extent, the truthfulness of a book or other information can be judged on its systemicity and the mutual connectivity of its content.

How Was This Book Written?

The content of this book goes far beyond established concepts and knowledge, but it is not a creation of my imagination at all. Some worldwide bestselling authors can write surprising fantasy novels manifested from their incredible imaginations, but this book is beyond the extent of even such writers' imagination. Some readers might immediately notice that this book could be written only when the writer's consciousness is beyond the earth and takes a completely cosmic view of a tremendous event of the universe—the Gaia Project.

Many readers may wonder how this book could have been written. Some readers who are familiar with channeled books may guess that this book was channeled, too. However, that is not the case. Though some channeled books provide surprisingly detailed explanations of cosmic events and life in space, perhaps no book that has been channeled is as systematic or self-sustaining as this book is.

This book was surely produced through my brain, but it is based neither on my imagination nor on channeling. Instead, the original Korean-language version of this book was written in a very unique way over a period of just one month. It is certainly not easy to explain the writing process convincingly—perhaps even to ascetic devotees who understand the invisible world and have had their own spiritual experiences. However, it seems desirable to provide as detailed an explanation as possible regarding how the book was written in order to help readers understand how the Gaia Project is proceeding.

In December 2002, after publishing my first book, *What We See is Not the Only Truth*, I suddenly received several messages regarding my second book. These messages came from different beings and in different ways—including channeling, vivid dreams, and direct "energy reading," all of which indicated that I would write a new book. After receiving the messages, however, I had no idea what kind of book I would write, so I could not write anything at all. In the autumn of 2004, I began to receive messages regarding the book again, this time through channeling. In late March of 2005, I received a specific message that I should be ready to write a book within a week.

Although I still did not have any concrete ideas about the new book even after receiving the last message, I sat in front of my computer and waited for my fingers to move. The type of automatic writing that some channelers have experienced did not happen to me. Instead, I felt a definite connection to a special energy through my seventh, or "crown," chakra.

From that time on, I was in a state of continuous inspiration, and numerous records of earth and the universe stored in my aura were surfacing one by one. During the writing, this newly revealed knowledge, which was mostly astonishing even to me, was combined with the existing knowledge and realizations I had achieved as a result of my continuous self-awakening and the special spiritual experiences, including past-life regressions, that I'd had during the past several years. By rearranging my vast knowledge of the Gaia Project systematically, I completed the manuscript in a very short period of time.

As some readers may have already surmised, this book was planned a long time ago by the Project headquarters to help the Guides of the Project to awaken and to help the general public prepare for the earth's Great Change. I was designated to write the book, and I simply completed writing the book at the right time with the guidance and help from *Shin-myeongs*.

Although there are various possible ways to awaken people during the last period of the Gaia Project, reading this book and coming to an understanding of the Project is essential. When people begin to accept the contents of this book, not by their efforts but through the natural process of understanding, they will start to awaken and realize who they really are, what they have been doing on the earth, what will happen on the earth, and what they can achieve during the period of the Great Change.

As described above, I learned everything I have explained in this book through a natural process, and I organized and put all of it into this book. In this way, the most unusual book ever written in human history was completed. I expect that many readers who were open to believing the contents of this book at the beginning will realize that the information in this book is true, and especially so as people witness social chaos and as they experience big events on the earth that they had never before imagined.

Beyond Preconceived Notions

As discussed before, the most important preparation for the earth's Great Change is to read and understand this book as well as possible. In addition to understanding this book, however, it is also important for people to recognize and dismantle their preconceived notions. As readers now know, the expansion of consciousness should be the only concern for all of the beings on the earth. Apart from the Guides, whose main purpose for coming to this planet was to carry out missions related to the Gaia Project, all the beings who have lived on the earth came here in order to learn through experiences. The earth's Great Change will ensure that the last phase of the Gaia Project will be the best opportunity human beings have to expand their consciousnesses.

To utilize the Great Change as their best learning opportunity, people should know that perhaps the biggest obstacles to expansion of human consciousness are the preconceived notions they possess. Preconceived notions are defined as either frames for viewing the world or inherent ways of thinking. These notions limit the free thinking of human beings and narrow the scope of their thinking. All societies are filled with all kinds of belief systems, which are crammed into people's brains in the name of morality or codes of conduct.

Such belief systems present standard societal judgments about what is and what is not advisable in all human behaviors and in all kinds of relationships, such as those between married partners, between parents and children, and between friends, neighbors, bosses and subordinates, and so on. Also, notions of gender or aesthetics are mostly formed from childhood, and notions of religion are usually forced on us by parents or religious people. All these societal ideas have a very powerful influence on our lives.

Most of these preconceived notions are formed in the home and in the schoolroom, and they are usually intended to make a person into a more excellent student, a more successful career builder, or a more respected citizen. When an individual's values or ways of thinking are in accord with general societal belief systems, that person can more easily adapt to the realities of life. However, when a person's personal value system conflicts with such societal belief systems, then he or she cannot easily adapt to material life on the earth, which results in complications and pain.

In this way, preconceived notions play a role in carrying on material life smoothly, but they also become the biggest constraint on the expansion of consciousness—since they limit human experiences and interfere with free thinking. Let us take an example of an individual who is very well equipped with morality. At the moment that individual encounters something new, he or she unconsciously, based on preconceived societal norms, makes a judgment about it. Such a person demarcates strictly what should be done and what should not be done using these preconceived ideas.

It is notable that social belief systems such as morality and codes of conduct are not based on a person's own experiences, but rather on the thinking and judgments of others. Thus, living a life following ready-made societal norms is exactly the same as giving your life to other people. That is, if people live their lives strictly controlled by societal expectations, then they cannot really live their own lives, since they will have no experiences of their own with which to expand their consciousnesses. Even if the notions are not forced on someone, but formed within oneself, the effect on spirituality is still the same. Since a person with pre-conceived societal notions perceives and judges the present situation as something similar to a past experience, the new experience cannot be accepted as it is.

Among various types of set ideas, the most serious threat to expanding consciousness comes from existing notions of spirituality. The invisible world that cannot be recognized through the five senses of the physical human body is not clearly perceived unless a person has special faculties. And even the information delivered by people with spiritual abilities is mostly inaccurate. Various religions and spiritual groups have espoused as doctrine such unreliable information. Once fixed ideas about spirituality are formed into religious doctrines, it is not easy for a follower of a religion to accept any new spiritual information, knowledge, or experiences that are not in line with those fixed ideas. Thus, new experiences and a new expansion of consciousness are suppressed.

The consciousness of each individual becomes locked in a limited space and chained up by those preconceived ideas due to many such notions. The more powerful the set ideas that people have, the more their consciousnesses are tied up in a narrow space. In this respect, people can be said to be slaves to their own set ideas. Consciousness expands gradually when people unchain themselves from their own inherent belief systems. Consciousness becomes more active and freer each time a person breaks away from a societal norm. If a person is free of all set ideas, the consciousness of the person may expand to the whole universe and that person may become completely free.

During the period of the Great Change, humans will witness many unusual events. If people are still armed with various preconceived ideas and judge the events of the Great Change based on those ideas, they will not get beyond the deep grief and anger caused by the events, and they will experience no expansion of consciousness. On the other hand, if people are ready to let go of their existing beliefs about the world, then they will be in a totally different situation. When an unprecedented event occurs, individuals may initially feel the same emotions—such as frustration, grief, or anger. However, once people start to discard their set ideas and begin to seek new meaning in the situation instead of judging it based on their existing belief system, their new experiences will begin.

When you get rid of your old ideas, then new concepts and new information can be recognized as actual possibilities instead of being rejected outright, and a new interpretation of the event becomes possible. That is, instead of immediately judging the events occurring during the Great Change as catastrophes or disasters, people may start to develop new interpretations of the events and find new meaning in them, leading to an expansion in consciousness. In this respect, removing preconceived notions one by one must be a very important part of each individual's preparation for the earth's Great Change.

Apparently, removing preconceived notions is not at all easy for anyone, especially for people who consider their belief systems to be part of their identity. However, you can begin the process of dismantling your set ideas by watching your mind and behavior carefully. You will first find yourself making instant judgments of various events as being either "good" or "bad." The criteria for judging things and occurrences are formed by the preconceived ideas you possess. Once you understand that, then you may begin to also understand that you are actually surrounded by and tied to numerous set ideas—and that you are tightly under their control, contrary to your expectations that you are living your own life with your own free will.

When you find that most of your beliefs were not formed within yourself but rather were inherited from people around you, then you will begin to realize that until now you have not lived your own life; rather, you have lived someone else's life. If you find that there is no universal value in your inherited belief systems, and that your free thinking and expansion of consciousness have been hindered by such set ideas, you will be ready to dismantle your preconceived notions one by one.

As discussed before, preconceived notions provide a framework to help a person adjust smoothly to society. Thus, as long as you still have a desire to live an abundant or happy life materialistically, the process of breaking down or getting rid of your set ideas may not be easy under normal circumstances. However, sooner or later you will find yourself in an unusual situation, a situation in which your priorities in life may change from having material abundance to understanding the real meaning of your life.

That will be the time for you to start the full-scale dismantling of your preconceived ideas. Before that, however, you need to firmly grasp the meaning of inherited ideas and their influence on your life and spiritual growth. This understanding may come naturally through meditation, spiritual practices, or as a result of reading spiritual books, including those in the recommended reading list in the appendix of this book. However, such an understanding will come most certainly by repeatedly reading this book and having a good understanding of the Gaia Project.

The Meaning of Spiritual Practices

Many spiritual seekers have considered special practices such as meditation and energy work to be detached from everyday life, and such people generally give such so-called spiritual practices priority over everything else in life. Seeking spirituality without falling prey to the material world can mean, of course, that a person's consciousness is quite different from that of the general public. However, as discussed in chapter 8, those who regard spiritual practices as the only important matter in life do so as a result of a serious misunderstanding of human life on the earth. Each and every moment of life on the earth is for learning, so everyday life itself is indeed a form of spiritual practice. An expansion of consciousness or spiritual growth can happen not only through spiritual practices, but also from everyday life. Every experience happening to a human being offers the opportunity for consciousness expansion. For the general public, daily life perhaps brings greater spiritual growth than specifically spiritual practices.

Of course, spending a whole lifetime devoted to intense and ascetic spiritual techniques and practices may be a good idea for the people who had already planned to do so before this life. Yet if one's situation does not allow sufficient time and money for spiritual practices but one is still obsessed with them, a large number of learning opportunities in life will be missed. A person who misunderstands spiritual practices due to preconceived notions about them, or due to an obsession with them, will not be able to focus on every moment of life and will not have any intense life experiences.

Ascetic devotees always speak about enlightenment, which is considered to be the ultimate goal of life. Although various truth seekers hold very different concepts or interpretations of enlightenment, each of these concepts may indicate a special *gi* (energy) experience. Such an experience sometimes comes to a spiritual devotee privately or slowly, or as a sudden change of the body and mind accompanied by various spiritual experiences. The common denominator in both cases is that the person's energy state changes fundamentally, a huge expansion of consciousness occurs, and—most importantly—an awakening of oneself takes place.

Along with a clear realization that all beings are connected to the Origin of the universe and that everything in the universe originates from one source, a person who undergoes this awakening experiences almost perfect peace for a while. For a person who recognizes only the third-dimensional world under the material shell, it is a special experience when one's *hyeol*—the acupuncture points of the body—are opened and one's mind is connected to the fourth-dimensional energy or higher that surrounds us.

Enlightenment, which is often called emancipation or salvation, can be understood as a state of being that is free from one's material disguise. Although some ascetic or spiritual devotees interpret it as having the wisdom to see through the universe or as the completion of human development, this interpretation is far from accurate. Among people who have had an enlightenment experience, there are some who gradually begin to understand the truth of the universe and who, thanks to their high original frequencies, do so by connecting to the energies of the fifth dimension or higher. But in most cases, people begin to approach their consciousness at the fourth and, later, the fifth-dimensional frequency by connecting to the third- and fourth-dimensional energies of the earth. In this respect, ascetic spiritual practices can be interpreted as techniques that are used to perceive the invisible fourth-dimensional world, and enlightenment can be regarded as the state of having a clear understanding of the existence of the fourth-dimensional world while being ready to move on to the fifth dimension.

Seeing enlightenment from this perspective, you will understand that ascetic practices or spiritual enlightenment are merely some of the many earthly experiences that one can have, especially in the case of beings with higher than fourth-dimensional frequencies who have come to the earth for various reasons. Due to the memories of high-dimensional worlds in the universe, which transcend the material world, such beings often show a tendency to be drawn into spirituality and to become attached to enlightenment, since they are not easily satisfied with the reality of material life. However, even though they experience enlightenment, it is still not possible for them to increase their current frequencies above their original frequencies or to attain a special state of consciousness that they have never before reached.

On the other hand, steps toward enlightenment can be the most important goal of most people's lives. To achieve this goal, it is most important to maximize one's experience while focusing on each moment of life with an open mind. An immediate judgment about something new, which is made based upon preconceived notions and existing knowledge, results in interference with the new experience. If a person does not focus on each moment but worries instead about the past or future, the intensity of the experience is weakened and an expansion of consciousness cannot properly take place.

Expansion of consciousness takes place gradually through direct experiences. Spiritual seekers often feel that a great expansion of consciousness takes place all at once—for instance, while meditating or while reading a spiritual book. However, such an experience is not a genuine expansion of consciousness, but only a feeling caused by the recovery of the person's original consciousness level. Being touched by certain spiritual books is a phenomenon during which the contents of the books resonate with the person's accumulated inner memories. Such an experience helps to recover a person's original level of consciousness, but it never provides a new experience or a new expansion of consciousness.

To undergo a true expansion of consciousness, it is above all necessary to observe your own preconceived beliefs and to recognize the problems associated with them. A shortcut to consciousness expansion is to recognize every preconceived notion you have and to break them all down one by one. Since the breaking down of preconceived ideas broadens the working space for your consciousness, breaking them down one by one should be a matter of highest priority. During the process of breaking down your set beliefs and of opening your mind to the outside world, the extent of your recognition naturally widens. By gradually moving away from self-centered thinking, your interests—which were formerly focused only on people such as parents, siblings, and friends—extend to your neighbors and even to the your entire nation and to all humanity. You also come to care about non-human life forms, and to more easily accept the existence of extraterrestrials and UFOs.

It is most important that everyone living on the earth at this moment rise above preconceived ideas, and look at the world with an open mind. Doing so is not only necessary for the general public, which has recognized only the material world so far, but it is perhaps even more necessary for people who think that they have already achieved enlightenment through long ascetic practices or who think they already know much about spirituality. Usually, people who have undertaken much spiritual practice are encased in a more solid shell, so it is much more difficult for them to break the shell and get out of it. Their religious precepts, their spiritual experiences, and the knowledge they have acquired have not only created this very solid shell in combination with their spiritual egos, but such people also feel comfortable inside their shells, and they do not even realize that they are trapped in such a small space.

It is necessary for such people to see what the enlightenment they have experienced really means—whether that enlightenment is about the universe in general or if it is just limited to the earth. They need to examine whether what they think they know is really, in fact, just a clumsy assemblage of knowledge from various books. If a person's knowledge can explain all of the phenomena of this world systematically and consistently, it might be the truth of the universe. If not, the person needs to get out of his self-created shell and look at the world from a different point of view.

What Can Be Done Now?

As mentioned before, the best preparation for the Great Change is to take in the Gaia Project, not by your efforts to believe in it but through your understanding. If you are open-minded toward the possibility of a world completely different from conventional ideas, you may take time to quietly contemplate yourself and this world. You may flip matters around to see if there are any hidden worlds you have neglected to see, take on a whole new perspective, and see the fundamentals of the world in a different light. You will then begin to feel the invisible world along with the physical world, and to understand that this invisible energy world is, in fact, the real essence of our world. From this moment of realization, the extent of your knowledge regarding life and the universe will expand rapidly, and you will begin to understand this book much more easily, deeply, and richly—and hence be ready for the Great Change.

On the other hand, if you are not open to new ideas and you stick instead to existing knowledge and preconceived notions or religious doctrines, you may not recognize any signs of the Great Change and you will soon experience extreme anxiety, uncertainty, fear, and frustration. To open yourself to new ideas and new concepts, you should, first of all, think about how reliable or trustworthy the existing knowledge is, how many preconceived notions you have, and how much influence they exert on your life. If you find that you have been indeed tied down with numerous preconceived notions, then you can start to remove them one by one. Also, by understanding that existing knowledge, including so-called common sense, is not reliable at all, you will be able to open your mind to new concepts and new messages, and be prepared to accept the possibility of the Gaia Project.

The change described above is very fundamental—and, for most people, such a change may never happen in normal circumstances. However, such a change will come to many people in this period of time, especially when they begin to witness mass destruction and the collapse of the material world. In addition, the ever-increasing frequency of the earth's vibration will help tremendously to change people's focus of life from material happiness to spiritual growth because this increasing frequency will make people's chakras and *kyeong-hyeols* open easily, and hence will help humanity to recognize the invisible energy world.

Living a life following your inner feelings is also very important during this special period. As we experience every moment of life, our focus should be neither on the past nor on the future, but always on the present moment. Each and every person in a human body planned this present life before birth. In the planning process, what kind of experiences you would gain and what you would learn were carefully planned before you came into the material earth. In particular, all beings reincarnated at this time have articulated plans on how to spend their time during the last stage of the Gaia Project. Thus, living a life in accordance with the original plan has been and continues to be the best thing to do.

Since one's original life plan can be detected through deep inner feelings, which should be very subtle initially but become stronger later, it is important to live a life following your deep inner feelings. Such feelings are quite different from any desires based on your physical body—for example, desire for fame, richness, or physical beauty—or any thoughts generated by your mental processes. Although it is often difficult to differentiate inner feelings from your desires or your thoughts, especially when you always think with your brain and have strong life desires, you may start to detect your inner feelings while you watch yourself at every moment.

Various spiritual practices—including meditation, *gi*, or yoga—may be helpful in order to make you feel the existence of the invisible world and to expand your consciousness beyond the material earth. It is likely that, with spiritual practices, you will accept the possibility of the Gaia Project more easily. On the other hand, through such practices, your spiritual egos could also grow and your shell could be hardened. In addition, you are likely to be exposed to inaccurate knowledge or misleading beliefs about the world. Thus, it is important to fully understand the limitations and problems of spiritual practices if you choose to undertake them.

CHAPTER TEN
Cosmic Blessing on the Earth

Until now, the earth has been operated as a special place for learning. This school has accepted all applicants as its students, and allowed them to learn through their own experiences. The school has had a dual structure: one for actual practice sessions—and the other for reviewing the past, resting, and planning for the future.

The actual practice sessions occur in one large undivided room, where each student wears a disguise covering their whole body and gets diverse and intensive experiences in a state of complete oblivion regarding their past. Most learning for students occurs during the sessions in this practice room.

Once a practice session for a student is over, he or she leaves the practice room, and enters the other part of the school, taking off the disguise. Quite distinct from the intensity and competitiveness of the practice room, the atmosphere of the place outside the room is relaxed and filled with love. Here, students take a rest and prepare for the next practice session.

Based on the characteristics of students—including original frequency levels, types of disguises in the previous practice session, preferences, tendencies, and so on—each student is stationed in one of many rooms for different purposes or different activities. In particular, there are all sorts of preparation spaces for the next practice session.

From outside of the practice room, students can look at the activities in the practice room whenever they wish, but there is no way for students in an actual practice session to see outside the room. Thus, most of the students in the practice session do not even know of the existence of the place outside the room.

Recently, among students in the practice room, rumors have been gradually spreading about the existence of this other place, but most students still neither believe in its existence nor are interested in the rumor itself. Without noticing at all that they are actually students and involved in a practice session to learn through experiences, they think that the practice room is the only place that exists in the world. And they devote themselves to becoming materialistically richer.

Long ago, the school headquarters decided to shut down this special school and to change it into a general upper-grade school, in which only the applicants who have reached a certain level of learning will be accepted as students. To carry out this transformation smoothly and effectively, many preparations have taken place since that decision. One of the important preparations is to clean and dismantle the existing facilities including the practice room as well as other rooms.

This dismantling job began with the rooms outside the practice room, but now work has begun in the practice room, too. Due to the recent job of stripping down some portion of the interior of the practice room, the whole atmosphere of the practice room seems to have become tense. Now it is almost time for the whole practice room to be torn down.

Though some students inside the practice room sense that something unusual is going on, most of them still ignore the signs, thinking them to be nothing serious. However, all the other students outside the practice room were notified about the school closing long ago. While packing up and waiting for their departures, many of them are wondering about which school in the galaxy will be most suitable for them. In the sky over the school, many space vehicles are standing by to transport them to their different destinations.

Until not long ago, students who had finished their learning in the practice room were guided to the outside of the practice room. But now the passage from the practice room to the outside has been closed, so students who finish their practice sessions are guided to the space vehicles floating over the school. As the administrators of the school and the students are moving around busily, a rather disorderly atmosphere can now be sensed.

So far, the administrators of the school have made much effort to help each individual student. There were several occasions in the past when the practice room was totally or partially torn down or flooded in one morning in order to chase all of the students out of the room. This time, so that students in the practice room can have the greatest experience for learning, the school buildings have been torn down gradually and many events other than a sudden collapse have been introduced by the school administrators.

Through these careful preparations for the departing students, great learning will be achieved from the school's closing. Individuals will have enough time to realize that the school was part of an elaborate plan of the universe, a plan allowing beings to learn through vivid experiences, to know why they have stayed on the earth until now, and to understand what is really happening. Besides, after carefully considering the learning level and the preferences of each student, the school management is helping students to find appropriate new schools in order to ensure that all beings will undergo the most effective learning at their new schools.

Above is the current status of the earth expressed metaphorically, all of which I have tried to explain so far in this book. It is very different from what the general public believes and very different from existing knowledge among spiritual seekers, but it is quite an accurate explanation of the earth. This explanation may not seem acceptable to many people who until now have recognized only the material world, but it is the genuine picture of the earth and life on the earth, and of the earth's current situation.

If people ignore these facts, keep their materialistic thoughts, and stick to their existing religious frameworks, the earth's Great Change will come with great discomfort for them. For people who grant absolute value to physical life or who interpret the earth's Great Change as a catastrophe, the coming enormous physical changes will bring indescribable anxiety and fear as the Great Change progresses. As people witness small and large buildings collapsing together like toys and land caving in while relatives and friends die from mysterious diseases, they will run about in confusion, trying to find a way to live.

However, there is no perfect "shelter" from the earth's Great Change for anyone. Those who have some understanding of this book or about how the universe moves should know that there is no such thing as a great final catastrophe, and hence no need to escape from such a catastrophe either.

It is very important for every person on the earth to realize the true meaning of life, the universe, and the earth's Great Change. It is just a complete waste of time to wander about trying to find a safe place to avoid the catastrophe. It is also important to know that it will be of no help to anyone to try to know when, where, and what is going to happen in the future, or to try to predict in advance what will happen. There is no possibility whatsoever of knowing in advance the specific events that will take place during the Great Change. If such information were open to the public, it would be nothing but a great obstacle to the smooth execution of the project and to the leap in consciousness of humankind. Therefore, if anyone says they are providing a detailed time and location of natural disasters, it is incorrect information and of no meaning at all.

The Preparation Period

From the beginning of the Gaia Project, the Great Change of the earth was planned as the last phase. Since the main purpose of staying on the earth for the residents was to learn through experiences, the Great Change was planned as a cosmic festivity, in which the graduating students will have last-minute special experiences, which can lead them to a leap in consciousness. According to the plan, people will initially suffer greatly from the total collapse of everything that they have relied upon for so long, but will then experience great joy, absolute peace, and gratitude toward the Origin by realizing who they really are and why they have been here on the earth. This process will happen to all people who open their minds to new possibilities.

To make these festivities possible, a great deal of preparation was necessary for quite a long period of time. In particular, it was necessary to loosen some strict rules for administrating the physical world. In order for effective learning to take place, the operating system of the earth has been kept top secret, so that almost no one would notice that the earth is actually a special school. However, to make the final festivities possible, it became desirable to reveal some of the secrets of the earth little by little and to give people some hints regarding the true meaning of life on the earth.

For this purpose, first of all, some of the strict rules of reincarnation have begun to be mitigated. Up until this decision was made, the memories of previous lives were completely blocked at the time of reincarnation except in a few cases. After the decision, however, some people began to perceive somewhat vaguely the existence of the spiritual world and the reincarnation system. Some ascetic devotees had glimpses of their past lives and the spiritual world during meditation or through ascetic practices. As many more people were allowed to develop their spiritual senses and spiritual abilities, some had a glimpse of the true features of the earth, which is composed of the dual structures of one spiritual world and one material world.

During the latter half of the nineteenth century, new perspectives on the world such as Theosophy appeared, and the New Age movement also began. As new methods of seeking the truth and new ways of thinking regarding God and the universe surfaced, more and more Western people moved away from the traditional Christian religion, which teaches salvation only through Jesus Christ and the Christian church. At the same time, understanding of past lives and reincarnation began to spread. Edgar Cayce, by reading the past lives of many people and by healing so many illnesses based on his readings, greatly influenced people in the West and led many to accept the fact of past lives and reincarnation.

In addition, many monks of Lamaism, including the Dalai Lama, went into exile after the Chinese invasion of Tibet, which provided an opportunity for Western people, through exposure to Tibetan Buddhism, to study and accept the idea of reincarnation. Furthermore, many spiritual devotees who already acknowledged the existence of past lives came to have a stronger belief in reincarnation when they saw their past lives vividly either in dreams or during meditation.

Recently, the existence of previous lives and reincarnation has begun to be known in another way—that is, as a result of past-life regressions through hypnosis. Despite continuing disputes about its authenticity, re-experiencing past lives through hypnosis has totally changed the viewpoints of many people toward life. During a past-life regression, experiencers do not merely view events in their past lives from the standpoint of a third person, but they actually vividly re-experience even the very emotions of each moment they are remembering. Through such an experience, a strong self-awakening regarding the true meaning of life occurs, and their lives change fundamentally.

In recent years, many people have had near-death experiences that involve remembering what happened to them after they were medically pronounced dead. These special experiences are happening to so many people all over the earth now, awakening them to accept the world after physical death and to realize the true meaning of life. Also, many people have come to perceive the existence of *gi* (the energy of the universe) and to recognize the invisible world through the Eastern practices of *gi* or yoga, which have become more popular all over the world.

Moreover, a considerable number of channelers have recently appeared who can communicate with various spiritual beings. These channelers are able to deliver messages from various beings in the invisible world. It is true that most of the messages delivered through channelers are not from beings in very high dimensions, but instead are mostly from third- or fourth-dimensional beings or even from thought forms created by humans. Thus, the messages and information delivered has often been either inaccurate or distorted. Besides, some of the channelers receiving the messages have not been well prepared for their jobs, so some of the messages have also been distorted by their impure minds. However, with regard to awakening people to expand their consciousnesses and to prepare for the earth's Great Change, the channeling phenomenon itself, as well as the overall message from the channelers, is very meaningful.

So far, the main messages received through channeling have been that a great change is coming to the earth, that the earth will ascend to the fifth dimension, and that each individual's emotional energy will be purified or released. Although there have been cases in which some spiritual devotees have accepted all the messages through a channeler as truth and as a result have become totally confused about life and the universe, channeled messages have been playing an important role in the Great Change.

The appearance of many UFOs or space vehicles is also awakening many people. UFOs have been seen by many people throughout the world, especially during the latter half of the twentieth century. These sightings have helped people to think about the possibility of other worlds outside of the earth and to expand their consciousness beyond the material earth. As time passes, the number of people who witness UFOs, along with the number of people who have reportedly been contacted by the space vehicles, is increasing geometrically.

Some UFOs from certain stars have made thousands of huge mysterious patterns in fields, known by humans as "crop circles," during the past twenty years. These crop circles, which appear overnight mostly on the plains of Europe and South America, are very shocking to the general public, not only because they are elaborate and beautiful, but also because they consist of intricate geometric symbols. Because of their size and characteristics, it is difficult for anyone, even people who do not accept anything about the invisible world, to believe that the crop circles were created by humans.

So far, many different types of evidence and phenomena suggest the existence of a world beyond the material earth. If people begin to open their minds a little to the possibility of the invisible world, their previous beliefs about the material world and their way of thinking that centers around the earth and human beings will easily be broken down.

As further preparation for the final festivities, the emotional memories stored in each person's aura have begun to be released either through personal experiences or at social events. The emotional energy of individuals—caused by such feelings as sorrow, rage, envy, jealousy, and hatred—piles up due to their various experiences in life. If such emotional energy is continuously accumulated without any resolution, people will fall into a state of anxiety. For that reason, a state caused by emotional energy must be resolved at a certain point in time. The accumulated emotional energy must be removed and purified not only from the current life but also from past lives. Such resolution of energy from the past can usually be completed by meeting beings from previous lives again and experiencing the opposite situation with them. Through this karmic process, the emotional energy piled up in one life will be resolved.

However, the material earth is being shut down, and so the possibility of a future life in which to resolve karma no longer exists. For this reason, accumulated emotional energy has recently been gushing out of people in many ways, regardless of whether or not they are aware of it. The resolution of energy can be completed by experiencing discord, agony, or pain from relationships with other people, and by experiencing severe emotional ups and downs.

The energy can also be resolved through a collective social event. For example, some energy from bitter or sad memories is released by shouting during political gatherings or by hurling stones at police during street demonstrations. Some emotional energy can also be released by weeping, laughing, or screaming while watching a sporting event among a huge crowd in a stadium or while watching a movie in a cinema. In these ways, our emotions are being purified.

In this process, mass media—including movies—have effectively helped to accomplish the collective resolution of accumulated energy and the breakdown of preconceived notions. For example, the movie *The Matrix* gave a hint that life is planned. By helping people to break down the clear division between imagination and reality, the *Harry Potter* books and movies have played a role in reducing the impact that the earth's coming ascension into the fifth dimension will have.

The Lord of the Rings movies hinted at the ordeal that all of humankind will experience before the advent of the new era, as well as at the united kingdom of harmony and prosperity that will be laid out afterward. Many movies about disasters on the earth, such as *Independence Day*, *Deep Impact*, *Armageddon*, and *The Day After Tomorrow*, have warned people in advance about the catastrophes the earth will experience during the purification process. Also, the movie *The Passion of the Christ* suggested that this world is operated not by humans but rather for a specific purpose of the universe, and it forced us to ask ourselves whether we would be able to recognize a holy person if one actually showed up among us right now.

The Last Days of the Earth

All beings on the earth—humans, animals, plants—are now spending their final moments here. These words can also be applied to the beings who will stay on the earth even after its ascension to the fifth dimension, because the fifth-dimensional earth will be a completely different world from the current earth. Therefore, for all the beings of the earth, including you and me, this moment is the last moment to spend on the third-dimensional material earth.

Before beginning this life, everyone went through the process of evaluating their accumulated experiences and planning this life. In particular, all of us planned how we were going to experience the earth's Great Change. For anyone who has a Higher Self in the fifth or higher dimension, the Subordinate Self on the earth will be reunited with the being above sometime after the earth's Great Change. According to what was already planned before this life, anyone who rises to the fifth dimension has the choice of either staying on the earth after its Great Change or moving to some other world in the fifth-dimensional universe. For beings whose consciousnesses are lower than the fifth dimension, it has already been decided that they will move to other worlds that suit their frequencies.

Since each being's course is already decided, the final farewell party, which has been prepared by the Gaia Project headquarters, has just begun. It is not the kind of party in which everyone gets drunk and disorderly while forgetting about their existence. Instead, it is one in which everyone recovers faint memories about themselves and prepares for the final times when everyone can accelerate spiritual growth. As the ground has already begun to tremble and the weather has already lost its stable patterns, this most precious time has come to all human beings, a time when they feel something lacking. All of the beings who have stayed on the earth through repeated reincarnations until now will soon be scattered all over the galaxy. The time for separation has just begun. Regardless of their level of consciousness or their mission, most of the beings who have been living on the earth will soon have to pack their bags and leave for a long trip.

As the separation time comes, people will have a moment for remorse and a moment to be united with the Origin of the universe. Whether we took good care of our neighbors or caused them pain, we all played our own roles in the mutual learning process, helping others to learn. People who treated me badly were in fact wonderful teachers. We have all worked hard to be each other's teachers, sharing good and bad times together, but the time for separation of all beings on the earth has come. We cannot remember it well yet, but at the moment we take off our physical human bodies, we will all remember everything in the past, and we will miss everything about the earth. Above all else, all of us will be self-awakened and realize that we all originated from one source in the beginning.

During the rest of the time we stay on the earth, no matter what happens to us or to the people around us, we should not simply look at a specific phenomenon, but rather observe its intrinsic nature. As we understand the profound meaning of the universe hiding behind the phenomenon, everything will change into joy. The real meaning of the earth's Great Change is not to give people sadness and pain through the collapse of the material earth, but instead to make people experience that sadness changes into joy and pain into gladness, and to awaken people to the understanding that all beings originated from one source. The universe will let us know that there is no reason to feel resentment or to blame anyone—because everything that happens to us is the result of our own choices. Through such self-awakening, we will have our chance for a leap in consciousness. That is the purpose of the earth's Great Change.

From Suffering to Bliss

Some spiritual seekers think humans are capable of creating or changing anything through the mind, but that is far from true. The earth's Great Change that is happening now cannot be stopped, changed, or postponed by anybody at the present time. It cannot be changed nor should it be changed. All changes taking place now are for the progress of the entire universe and for all beings of the universe.

I once spent quite a bit of time doing academic research on the stock market. When there are potentially unfavorable conditions for the stock market, such conditions tend to have a strong influence before they are fully revealed, but not afterward. Similar is the state of human mentality. No matter how unbearable something seems before it occurs, it becomes bearable for people when it ultimately happens. However, when people are anticipating a difficulty or are uncertain about whether or not a difficulty will actually come, they complain of great pain. It is the uncertainty that is most difficult for people to handle.

Human suffering is caused in part by materialism. The earth's Great Change will offer a special experience in that regard. Human beings will have the experience of losing everything that they thought they possessed, and they will learn the true joy of being free of possessions. When people realize that they do not own anything in the material world, all of their fear and anxiety will disappear and they will experience true peace of mind, a piece of mind that cannot be influenced by anything on the outside. No matter what happens, people will not fear any longer.

During the period of the earth's Great Change, individuals will find that certain things that they used to consider natural are no longer natural, and that their most strongly held beliefs are not correct. Such a realization will, of course, shake up preconceived notions and existing knowledge, both of which have so far manifested with such mighty power in people's lives; humans will now open their minds to all new possibilities. Human consciousness will be able to expand through the earth's Great Change in precisely this way.

Moreover, people who have taken advantage of others for their own benefit and profit will also undergo self-awakening. They will learn from the Great Change that they can no longer do just as they wish and that they are as helpless as anyone else. Through such a self-awakening, solidarity among people will be achieved. By realizing that they all originated from one source, individuals will recover their awe of the Origin of the universe, and their connectivity with the Origin will become concrete. In this respect, the Great Change will play the role of reconnecting each person with their origin, from which they have been seemingly cut off for so long.

If you are reading this book for the first time, you might now be worrying more about the future and feeling more anxiety. However, as you develop a greater understanding of the content and accept it, your anxiety will gradually disappear and your mind will begin to experience complete peace. To anyone who understands the earth, human beings, and the purpose of the Great Change, any approaching physical pain or difficulty will be bearable, and in fact will even bring great joy. This is true spiritual awakening and true enlightenment, which brings freedom, bliss, and peace of mind. True knowing gives us real freedom. This book was written with such an aim.

Before going to an actual practice session on the earth, beings need an orientation session explaining the purpose of the actual practice and what is necessary in order to get the best results from the practice. Similarly, this book provides the necessary orientation for all residents of the earth as we prepare for the Great Change. That is, with a clear understanding of this book, you will be fully prepared for all the coming events—and you can enjoy them, regardless of your original level of consciousness. When the time comes, you will gladly leave your physical body to travel to a new world.

The Final Message

This is the only guidebook of the earth's Great Change, which is in progress now. This is the alpha and the omega for resolving the numerous fundamental questions of life.

Here is all of the core truth that all the people living on the earth surely need to read and understand.

Do not compare this book to any other book or scriptures presented to the human world so far. If you are an intellectual, take one step back from your existing knowledge. If you are a religionist, take one step back from your existing religious notions. Then, read this book. When you do so, you will begin to feel whether what you already know is true or not and whether what you have believed until now is true or not.

If reading this book has made you very confused, it is very natural and not strange at all. The confusion has occurred simply because the knowledge and beliefs crammed into your brain have collided with your inner knowing. Such confusion is inevitable because this book has stimulated your true knowing, which is stored deep inside you, and the knowing revealed is still colliding with your existing knowledge and beliefs. Your inner self or the memories in your aura know what the truth is. Listen carefully to the sound inside.

If you are still confused, take your time and wait a little while. And then observe how the earth is changing and what is happening around you. Sooner or later, you will naturally come to know what this book is all about.

Questions and Answers

Following are the questions most frequently asked by readers since the publication of the Korean-language version of *The Gaia Project*, along with my answers.

Q1: Your book states that many people will suffer from or die from natural disasters, social chaos, wars, or mysterious diseases by the end of 2009. Is this true? If so, will our earnest prayers influence God to prevent these events? If these events are inevitable, could you tell us the details of what will happen?

A: What would you do if the world ended tomorrow? *The Gaia Project* is a book written while I was in a state of special energy; it is a book whose contents became clarified by my continuously flashing inspirations. It will be very meaningful for you to think why you have these questions. If I said that they are true, would you believe my words? What would you do if you accepted them as true? And what things would you do today if we were all going to die tomorrow?

Not only the answers to the questions you asked above, but also the answer to the inquiry "How should we live our lives?" is in the book. While readers with superficial understanding may not find the answers in the book, serious readers will be self-awakened.

Q2: You said that while you were writing The Gaia Project, you were in a state of special energy. From that statement, I get the impression that even if the contents of the book turn out to be false, you will not accept any responsibility. If so, I think it is irresponsible for you to disappoint those who sympathize with the plans of the universe revealed in The Gaia Project. If your statements turn out to be false, wouldn't it be a sorry situation for many people? In this regard, to resolve doubts and questions people may have, I think you need to tell us more about specific events and changes that will occur in the future, instead of simply saying, "Let's wait and see."

A: It seems very meaningful to think about responsibility. People like to use the word "responsibility" and they like to hear that word from others. When political leaders emphasize "responsibility" and behave accordingly, they are considered to be truthful and trustful. It is the same with spiritual leaders. However, taking "responsibility" physically may be possible for the people who recognize only the material world. If you understand the real meaning of life and existence, you will know that there is no way for one to take "responsibility" for someone else in any way. I can say that if one spiritual leader is speaking for "responsibility," either he does not know the real meaning of life or he or she is using that intentionally for a concealed purpose. By reading *The Gaia Project* over and over, you will completely get what I am saying about responsibility now.

As I often say, you do not have to make an effort to totally believe in the Gaia Project. Only accept it as much as you can and act accordingly. If one believes fifty percent in the Project, one should live up to that level of acceptance. People who act as if they accept the Project one hundred percent are simply being dishonest. This affectation is not proper. As I clearly state in *The Gaia Project*, only you yourself are responsible for your life. Please do not be deceived by a spiritual leader who asserts that he or she will take responsibility for your spiritual life.

The Gaia Project delineates not only the earth's Great Change, but also the various truths about life and the universe not found in any other book in the world. The important thing for people now is not to learn what events will happen and when they will occur. Rather, by opening your mind and accepting the possibility of the events described in the book, you focus on every moment of life and realize the truth piece by piece.

Q3: As people learn more about the earth's Great Change, some of them are changing their life plans, by canceling emigration plans or insurance plans, for example. Is changing one's life plans appropriate?

For the growth of our consciousness, wouldn't it be appropriate to live as we had planned?

A: Your inquiries concern the question, "How should we live at this moment?" As described in *The Gaia Project*, only you yourself are responsible for your life. If one becomes self-aware and aware of the future, and consequently walks a new path of life through *The Gaia Project* or my lectures, it would be a true blessing of the universe. If people around you try to stop you because of their concerns based on their own viewpoints on life, it would be meaningless and foolish. On the other hand, there may be people who do not have a firm belief or realization of the future, but who use the contents of *The Gaia Project* as an excuse for fleeing from reality.

Living life as planned originally would be best for every being on the earth. However, which paths in life are planned and which are not planned may never be clear for most people. And it is not wise to try and figure it out. Instead, just accept every reality you encounter and focus on every moment of life. If you are influenced somewhat by *The Gaia Project*, neither try to pretend that you are not influenced by the book nor overemphasize the influence on yourself or others. It may be best for you to live your life exactly as influenced.

Q4: I read that in the sky there are UFOs from the third-dimensional stars as well as from higher-dimensional worlds, but why aren't they visible? Also, can the scientific level of other third-dimensional worlds be so advanced as to travel many light years and reach the earth?

A: Most people cannot sense the third-dimensional frequency of the non-material world. What they perceive is only the materialized world. Since UFOs or space vehicles are usually in a non-material state, regardless of whether they are from a third-dimensional or a higher-dimensional world, we cannot catch them through any of our five senses.

It is incorrect to assume that a lower-dimensional world has a low-level civilization. Note that human civilization on the earth progressed to the current level in only thousands of years. In *The Gaia Project*, there are many astonishing stories. If you try to feel and think about them deeply while reading the book repeatedly, your consciousness will be rapidly expanded.

Q5: I don't understand why the Guides who will spread the earth energy to other stars need to take UFOs or space vehicles to reach them. Isn't a UFO unnecessary since a being without a physical body can fly to any star?

A: Beings of each star reorganize their energy bodies to make them suitable to the frequency of the star upon entrance. Since the earth is no exception, all beings on the earth have reorganized their energy bodies so that they can live here without any special equipment. (Beings on the earth mentioned above include various kinds of souls wandering around, such as human beings; beings in the spiritual world; and *Shin-myeong* sent by the Project head-quarters.)

On the other hand, earthly beings need special equipment in outer space. One of these pieces of equipment is a space vehicle. The vehicle enables a being to stay in the outer world without reorganizing its energy body; it basically has non-materialistic characteristics and materializes if needed.

When a being from another star visits the earth, it must use a space vehicle since its energy body doesn't fit the earth. In addition, the Guides who are to spread the earth energy to other stars will visit each star after they codify the corresponding information in their energy bodies.

Q6: You said that the earth consists of the third-dimensional material world and the fourth-dimensional spiritual world. I wonder how a second-dimensional being can exist in both of them.

A: In the universe, beings of the same dimension usually live together. When required by the universe, however, it is possible for beings of different dimensions to coexist. For example, although Sirius, the administrative center for the Gaia Project, is a sixth-dimensional star, beings of diverse dimensions can gather there for work because of the equipment available for adjusting dimensions.

The earth was originally formed to develop a unique energy to induce growth of consciousness of the whole universe, and to cultivate the energy's immune force. For the latter purpose, the earth was open to all beings of all dimensions so that they could live together. All living creatures on the earth possess special energy bodies or auras supporting their material bodies. Upon death, however, the energy bodies of all the beings are reorganized into other forms, so they can stay in the fourth-dimensional spiritual world.

Q7: You said that the kinesiology test used to distinguish truth from falsehood has its limits because one's mind could influence the outcome. Couldn't a double-blind test eliminate the influence of one's subjectivity?

A: Spiritual information, whether attained by a kinesiology test or by spiritual capability, is basically filtered through our mind. Mind plays the role of a mirror. Therefore, spiritual information can be accurate only if one has a completely cleansed mind, which figuratively has a smooth surface. Then, the mind can reflect things as they are without any distortion. As for most people, because the entire surface or a part of the surface of each person's mirror is uneven, the true image of an object cannot be reflected properly.

For the above reasons, it is almost impossible to expect one hundred percent accuracy from a kinesiology test or similar methods, even if one makes his or her mind calm and peaceful through meditation before the test. Despite their limitations, kinesiology tests or the use of L-rods—L-shaped rods used to detect underground water streams—are useful to expand one's understanding of the energy world.

Q8: Wouldn't the Gaia Project be more success-ful if more people experienced the earth's Great Change with an understanding of the true mean-ing of the Project? In addition, what is the relation-ship between the vaccine energy and each person's growth of consciousness?

A: Everyone should read about and learn the true mean-ing of the Project fully described in *The Gaia Project*. Not knowing the significance of the Project, one will lose a golden opportunity to expand one's consciousness. But the success of the Gaia Project does not rely on each person's growth of consciousness. The Project has already reached its final stage, and now nobody can stop it or hinder it. Although all beings on the earth have contributed to the for-mation of the vaccine, each being has come to the earth not for the Project but for the being's own growth of conscious-ness through unique earthly experiences. It is true that even if the experiences caused by the changes of the future will be very precious to an individual, one has the freedom to refuse it. However, it is essential that as many people as pos-sible know the real meaning of the earth's Great Change.

Q9: My understanding is that in the course of the earth's Great Change, most beings will leave the earth and move to other stars appropriate for their own dimensions and frequencies, since most will not be compatible with the frequency of the fifth-dimensional earth. Will family members of different dimensions part as well?

A: All beings on the earth have experienced meeting and parting through the reincarnation system, and the separation of family members during the period of the earth's Great Change will not differ from previous ones. I hope that you have an opportunity to observe yourself through the questions rising in your mind, and that you become aware of how restricted your thoughts are to the material world.

Q10: I feel that not only other spiritual groups but also the Gaia Project community expect many people to die by natural disasters and hope that this expectation is realized. Isn't this attitude a form of an apocalyptic idea?

A: The earth's Great Change in progress does not indicate the end of the world, but rather the rebirth of the earth to a higher dimension. During this transformation, many people will realize that they are brothers and sisters from one origin. To those who know that human beings are originally spiritual beings, the earth's Great Change can be recognized as "a blessing of the universe," not as a catastrophe.

Some spiritual psychics and religious or spiritual groups foresee apocalyptic calamity and assert that only they can "save" the people. However, they seem to make such claims to extend their power, using people's anxious minds, because they do not know the facts and the significance of the earth's Great Change. Neither an individual nor a group can "save" anyone else. The true meaning of the Great Change is to expand individuals' consciousnesses by self-awakening, so they realize that everything has resulted from their choices, and no one else and nothing else is to blame.

Unlike people who think that only visible things and the physical world are all that exist, those who understand the non-material world and the real meaning of life will not fear the earth's Great Change.

Q11: In the book *The Gaia Project*, there is some discussion about the negative aspects of existing religions. However, many people agree on some of the positive aspects of religious precepts. For example, such beliefs encourage people to love and care for their neighbors, and they lead people to a spiritual life rather than to indulgences in materialistic pleasure. What is your opinion on this issue?

A: It is true that many people recognize the positive effects of religions on human society and I am not totally against them. However, we see that this recognition of social contributions from religions comes from the standpoint of third-dimensional materialistic thought. Some religious precepts have greatly contributed to securing and maintaining society, but not necessarily to spiritual growth.

For example, the religious precepts' focus on individuals develops people's hypocrisy and double-faced personalities. Most religious precepts are based on the sayings of the saints; thus, they generally suggest the way that all beings should live. A problem is that instead of individuals' following such doctrines voluntarily with passion, precepts restrict other individuals, and there are social restrictions exercised over the individuals who do not follow the precepts. Thus, due to such precepts, a double-faced personality—showing discordance between one's mind and one's words or actions—has become a social virtue.

In addition, we can often hear a claim by some religious devotees that, for example, practicing such precepts for a long time can make one's desires that deviate from the precepts totally vanish or very much reduce. In appearance, this seems to be the case. However, in most cases, religious devotees' desires and hopes have merely submerged deep into their minds without being purged, and those will rise to the surface again when the chance permits.

Recommended Reading List

Brennan, Barbara Ann. *Hands of Light* (New York: Bantam, 1993).

Capra, Fritjof. *The Web of Life: A New Scientific Understanding of Living Systems* (New York: Anchor, 1997).

Cerminara, Gina. *Many Lives, Many Loves* (Camarillo, CA: DeVorss & Company, 1981).

Clow, Barbara Hand. *The Pleiadian Agenda* (Santa Fe, NM: Bear & Company, 1995).

Emoto, Masaru. *The Hidden Messages in Water* (Hillsboro, OR: Beyond Words, 2004).

Essene, Virginia and Sheldon Nidle. *You Are Becoming a Galactic Human* (Santa Clara, CA: S.E.E. Publishing Company, 1995).

Hancock, Graham. *Fingerprints of the Gods* (New York: Crown, 1995).

Hawkins, David R. *Power vs. Force: The Hidden Determinants of Human Behavior* (Carlsbad, CA: Hay House, 2002).

Jang, Hwee-Yong. *What We See Is Not the Only Truth* [in Korean] (Seoul, South Korea: Yang Moon Publishing, 2001).

Kerner, Dagny and Imre Kerner. *Der Ruf der Rose* [The Call of the Rose] (Cologne, Germany: Kiepenheuer & Witsch, 1994).

Montgomery, Ruth. *A World Beyond*, reissued edition (New York: Fawcett, 1985).

Moody, Raymond A. *Coming Back: A Psychiatrist Explores Past Life Journeys* (New York: Bantam, 1991).

Morgan, Marlo. *Mutant Message Down Under* (New York: Perennial, 2004).

Newton, Michael. *Journey of Souls* (St. Paul, MN: Llewellyn, 1994).

Phylos, Orpheus and Virginia Essene. *Earth, the Cosmos, and You: Revelations by Archangel Michael* (Santa Clara, CA: S.E.E. Publishing, 1999).

Radin, Dean. *The Conscious Universe: The Scientific Truth of Psychic Phenomena* (New York: HarperEdge, 1997).

Redfield, James and Carol Adrienne. *The Celestine Prophecy: An Experiential Guide* (New York: Warner, 1995).

Spalding, Baird T. *Life and Teaching of the Masters of the Far East* (Camarillo, CA: DeVorss & Company: 1986).

Talbot, Michael. *The Holographic Universe* (New York: HarperCollins, 1991).

Targ, Russell and Jane Katra. *Miracles of Mind: Exploring Non-Local Consciousness and Spiritual Healing* (Novato, CA: New World Library, 1998).

Tolle, Eckhart. *The Power of Now: A Guide to Spiritual Enlightenment* (Novato, CA: New World Library, 1999).

Tomkins, Peter and Christopher Bird. *The Secret Life of Plants* (New York: Harper and Row, 1973).

Wambach, Helen. *Life Before Life* (New York: Bantam, 1982).

Weiss, Brian L. *Many Lives, Many Masters* (New York: Simon and Schuster, 1988).

Weiss, Brian L. *Messages from the Masters* (New York: Warner, 2000).

Whitton, Joel and Joe Fisher. *Life Between Life* (Garden City, NY: Doubleday, 1988).

Glossary

Bon-tae-geuk: The original *tae-geuk*, which came from *mu-geuk*. It created the five consciousnesses of the Origin.

Chakra: Major energy centers in the human body, where physical and nonphysical bodies are connected. There are seven major chakras that are connected to seven layers of non-physical bodies (auras) respectively.

Consciousness: The essence of being. The faculty of a being that perceives the world and creates something out of it.

The Consciousness of the Origin; The First Consciousnesses in the Universe: The unified or the whole consciousness of the universe. They are the tenth-dimensional beings and there are five of them. These Original beings hold all the information throughout the universe with their exceedingly fast frequencies.

Dimension: A band of frequencies of vibration. The universe consists of ten dimensions, from the tenth dimension with the highest frequencies to the first dimension with the lowest frequencies. They coexist simultaneously. Even in the same dimension, there is quite a difference in frequency, so that a frequency can be classified by a dimension and also by a layer within a dimension.

Gaia: Another name for the earth, which comes from Greek mythology, referring to the earth goddess.

Gi: A metaphysical energy inherent in everything. Its unimpeded circulation and balance in the body are thought to be essential to good health in traditional East Asian medicine.

Guides: Beings with physical human bodies, who will reveal the will of the Origin during the earth's Great Change. They will undertake their missions through a manifestation of special spiritual abilities.

Gyeokam Nam Sagoh: A well-known Korean prophet in the seventeenth century.

Higher Self: Original beings in higher dimensions sometimes duplicate themselves for special purposes. In these cases, the original being is called the Higher Self, and the duplicated being who is sent to the earth or another lower-dimensional place is called the Subordinate Self or the Lower Self.

Hwan-in: The title of theocratic leaders of Hwan-kook. It means God. There were seven Hwan-ins in total.

Hwan-kook: The spiritual nation in Central Asia after the collapse of Lemuria. It originally meant "a country in bright light." This theocratic nation is known to have been a federation of twelve countries and had never sought material prosperity at all during its long history.

Hyeol: See *Kyeong-hyeol.*

Ilboo Kim Hang: A Korean philosopher in the nineteenth century. Insisting that the New Age had come, he invented a new philosophical system replacing the Book of Changes.

Jeungsan Gang Il Soon: A Korean saint in the late nineteenth century.

Kyeong-hyeol: *Gi* constantly circulates a human body vertically and horizontally. While *kyeong-rak* is the passage of it, *hyeol*, or *kyeong-hyeol*, is the major point on *kyeong-rak* near the skin where energies are exchanged between physical and nonphysical bodies. In traditional East Asian medicine, especially acupuncture, these points are used to resolve the impeded flow of *gi*. There are known to be fourteen *kyeong-raks* and three hundred and sixty *kyeong-hyeols*.

Lower Self: See *Higher Self.*

Maitreya: The future Buddha who is said to be reborn in a period of decline to renew the doctrine of Buddhism. After his rebirth, Maitreya is to lead all beings still trapped in the cycle of rebirths to Nirvana. His cult first appeared in India around the third century, and then spread throughout China, Korea, and Japan.

Materialization: The process of making the waves of a certain dimension have the nature of particles as well. Not only third-dimensional waves but also waves in other dimensions can be materialized. Once an energy world is materialized, the world begins to be recognized by the five senses of the physical human body. When the waves of lower dimensions are materialized, their appearance is more solid. The materialized world is only a small fraction of the whole universe.

Mu; Mooh: The Subordinate Self of the first consciousness of the universe, who has led the Guides and other beings from the beginning of Lemurian society. Along with many Guides and *Shin-myeongs*, this being of Origin will lead all the beings on the earth to a spiritual leap during the earth's Great Change.

Mu-geuk: The chaos from which *tae-geuk* was born. It is the state of nothingness and emptiness without any consciousness, but it has the potential of all conceptions.

Shin-myeong: The beings in energy body who work for the earth's Great Change. They awaken the Guides and make them ready for their missions at the planned time. They also do various work in the spiritual world of the earth.

Subordinate Self: See *Higher Self*.

Sukh vati: The Buddhist Elysium, a paradise.

Supporters: Human beings who support the Guides for the earth's Great Change, or do some activities for the Great Change. They work not with special spiritual ability but with their accumulated talent, knowledge, and recognizable social positions in the current life. Some of them are active spiritual leaders, healers, or internationally known best-selling authors.

Tae-geuk: The great absolute, the entity of the universe, and the origin of everything in the universe. It was the very first systematic power of the universe. According to Chinese cosmogony, it gives birth to yin (the negative) and yang (the positive), and the five elements (i.e., metal, wood, water, fire, and earth).

Taeho Bokhi (Fu His): The first Chinese emperor in the legendary age. He for the first time conceived *mu-geuk*, *tae-geuk*, and the eight trigrams that were used in the Book of Changes (I Ching) later. He is also known to have taught people fire cooking, net fishing, and taming animals.

Thought forms: Energy bodies that are created by human minds and that become active for specific goals. Their existence entirely depends on human minds. When people's desires become stronger or when more people participate in the activities creating and nourishing thought forms, their strength can greatly increase. On the other hand, they disappear when they are cut off from the human mind. Thought forms can either directly influence or even dominate people's thoughts, so they can cause some unexpected thoughts or unexpected behaviors in people.

Vaccine: The special ingredient that can convert earth energy to customized energy for each star in order to make the earth energy infiltrate into the energy of each star. To produce the vaccine, it was necessary for beings from all different dimensions and different layers of frequency to stay together on the earth, which is one reason why the earth was opened to all beings from the universe.

Index

False Self, 145
first consciousness of the universe, the, 17, 22, 24–25, 31, 45, 57, 69–70, 77, 148–150, 154, 239, 242
Fu His. *See* Taeho Bokhi

Gaia (Greek goddess), 14
gi (energy), ii, xi–xiii, 72, 104, 130, 156, 195, 202, 211, 240–241
globalization, 2
Goddess of Mercy, 89, 157
Great Change (period of change on the earth), xii, xv, 5–6, 11, 15, 27–28, 30–33, 35–36, 40–41, 48–51, 54–56, 62–63, 156, 165, 176–181, 188–189, 192–193, 199, 208–209, 212, 216–220, 225, 230–232, 240, 242–243
Great Floods, 86–87, 92, 99, 122
Guides (Gaia Project helpers), 11, 47–54, 56, 69, 76–77, 79, 88, 90, 121, 132, 138, 154, 188–189, 227–228, 240, 242–243
Gyeokam Nam Sagoh, 28, 240

Harry Potter (book series), 215
Hawkins, David, 165–166, 236

Higher Self, 22, 146, 154–156, 216, 240
Hwan-in, 79–80, 240
Hwan-kook, 78–80, 99, 241
Hwan-oong, 80
hyeol. *See* kyeong-hyeol

Ilboo Kim Hang, 28, 241
Incas, 68
Independence Day (film), 215

Jesus Christ, 18, 40, 87–88, 91, 112, 129, 157, 210
Jeungsan Gang Il Soon, 29, 241
John the Baptist, Saint, 129
John the Divine, Saint, 28

karma, 41, 56, 87, 91–92, 117, 122–125, 133, 152, 214
kinesiology, 229
Korea, ii. xv, 28, 30, 46, 78, 80, 131, 156, 223, 242
Korean Peninsula. *See* Korea
kyeong-hyeols, xi, 38, 103–104, 135, 196, 201, 241
kyeong-rak, 241

L-rod, xi, 229–230
Lamaism. *See* Dalai Lama
Lemuria, 33–36, 39, 48–50, 57, 69–71, 73–74, 76–80, 82–83, 85, 92, 96–97, 99, 122, 132, 140, 241–242
Lord of the Rings, The, 215
Lower Self, 154, 240